I'm grateful that Robin Jones Gunn has been both a longtime friend and a mentor because she has taught me in many ways how to gently lead my daughters into womanhood. I'm especially thankful that Robin's personal advice is now available to all! I highly recommend this book for all girl moms. I treasure the memories I've created with my daughters, and I know that others will too!

TRICIA GOYER
Speaker and *USA TODAY* bestselling author of more than seventy books

Moms today are hungry—hungry for help *and* hope, and thankfully Robin delivers both. In a world that tells you to dread adolescence and avoid difficult conversations, Robin casts a better vision—one that flips the script so you can celebrate your growing daughter, prepare her for reality, and help heal old wounds. Grounded in biblical truth, this book is honest and refreshing, helping you become the strong and intentional mom your tween daughter desperately needs!

KARI KAMPAKIS
Bestselling author of *Love Her Well* and *More Than a Mom* and host of the *Girl Mom* podcast

As a woman now in the "nana" stage of life, I can highly recommend *Before Your Tween Daughter Becomes a Woman* to grandmothers, too—or for grandparents to give to their daughters. Robin navigates the challenges and joys of raising a daughter with love and grace. I recommend this book with the highest praise!

JANET HOLM McHENRY
Author of twenty-five books, including *from Your Knees*

My years working as a youth minister did not fully prepare me to become the parent of a tweenaged daughter. I've watched her navigate the tensions of an international move, friendships, growing faith, and her changing body. I've not always had the words to say to encourage her well. *Before Your Tween Daughter Becomes a Woman* brought me to tears, giving voice to what I can't quite articulate as I watch my firstborn become a girl on the cusp of womanhood. Robin provides mothers like me the tools and confidence to nurture our daughters with intention. And as we watch them blossom, we are reminded of our own invitation to flourish well.

JENNY ERLINGSSON
Speaker and author of *Becoming His: Finding Your Place as a Daughter of God*

Robin Jones Gunn's *Before Your Tween Daughter Becomes a Woman* teaches moms how to honor and cherish their daughters so that their coming-of-age years can be marked by closeness and treasured moments instead of silence or awkwardness. Every mom should read this book, no matter her age, because it's never too late to let our daughters know the truth about womanhood—that we are each fearfully and wonderfully made. This book touched my heart, healed several emotional sore spots, and helped me think about ways to lovingly come alongside my daughter in these precious (and precarious) teen years. I loved reading it!

RACHEL DODGE
Author of *The Anne of Green Gables Devotional*, *The Little Women Devotional*, and *The Secret Garden Devotional*

Filled with creative and practical ideas, *Before Your Tween Daughter Becomes a Woman* is a great guide for moms everywhere. With her kind, personable writing style, Robin Jones Gunn does a fantastic job helping moms brainstorm ways to connect with their daughters while honoring our unique personalities and experiences. I can hardly wait to try many of these tips with my own tween daughter.

HILARY BERNSTEIN
Blogger, women's ministry director, and author of *Becoming a Modern-Day Proverbs 31 Woman*

I read Robin's book as a mother of a tween daughter and was moved to tears. My daughter and I struggle to connect at times, mostly because we are so different—and yet so alike. Helping her become a godly woman is my soul's cry, and this vulnerable and God-honoring book has given me direction to support my daughter in becoming a strong woman of faith. It's a strong recommend—a must-have for all mothers of tween daughters!

JAIME JO WRIGHT
Christy Award–winning author of *The House on Foster Hill*

before your tween daughter becomes a woman

a mom's must-have guide

Robin Jones Gunn

FOCUS ON THE FAMILY.

A Focus on the Family Resource
Published by Tyndale House Publishers

For the young women in my life

with much love

"Many women do noble things,
but you surpass them all."

PROVERBS 31:29

contents

foreword

Although my wife, Jean, and I don't have any daughters of our own (we were blessed instead with two sons), I have always believed that raising girls is a sacred trust. It's clear throughout Scripture that there is a special place in God's heart for His daughters, and parents have a weighty responsibility to protect, nurture, and cherish their precious girls. Moms, in particular, leave an indelible mark on their daughters' lives. Through their modeling, prayers, interactions, and wisdom, mothers are in a powerful position to influence the hearts, minds, and souls of their girls.

Many parents, however, are often blindsided when their children enter adolescence, and they're not always sure how to help guide their kids into this new phase of life in healthy, positive ways. It can feel awkward, uncomfortable, and even a little scary to address certain topics. Of course, there can be many legitimate reasons for this. Perhaps we're grieving what feels like the end of a child's innocence, or maybe we have difficult memories related to this period of time in our own lives. Or it could be that we simply don't know what to say. Whatever the reason, many parents feel ill equipped to broach the topic of puberty with their kids.

Not only that, but there is much confusion in today's culture surrounding the nature of true femininity, and these days some folks even seem to have trouble defining the word *woman*! In such a climate, it's no wonder that Christian parents of girls often feel overwhelmed by the task of raising daughters who will embrace their unique and God-given role as women in a broken world.

It's vital, however, for parents—and moms in particular— to take the initiative and engage with their daughters about what to expect as they move toward adulthood. Despite the unbiblical and somewhat bewildering messages society sends regarding what it means to be a woman, the good news is that God's Word has not changed. He still has a beautiful plan for womanhood, and even in a postmodern world girls can learn to reflect that unique design.

What do Christian parents want for their daughters? I believe that, above all, they want to raise young women who love Jesus and share that love with others. Part of that, of course, is for girls to understand the irreplaceable role they play in God's Kingdom work. They need to know that the Lord indeed values women, and that they have been "fearfully and wonderfully made" (Psalm 139:14). And as they prepare to come of age, young women should revel in the assurance that they have been specially created by a loving God for a divine purpose. They occupy a special and indispensable place in our world. They reflect God's character in a distinct way.

That's why I'm so excited about this book from Robin Jones Gunn. Robin is helping moms navigate a crucial turning point in their daughters' lives in a way that deepens the mother-daughter bond and ultimately points young girls to Christ and their Kingdom-building purpose.

Make no mistake—this isn't simply another "how to talk to your daughter about the birds and the bees" book. Instead, Robin wants to help you guide your daughter toward adulthood by honoring God's wonderful design for women. After all, girls can get *information* about puberty and sexuality anywhere, and in this day and age of ubiquitous technology, that kind of information is unfortunately theirs for the taking. A Christian mother, however, is in a wonderful position to share those specifics in ways that communicate her love for her daughter, God's sovereign anointing on her life, and what the Bible actually says about those crucial topics.

And don't we want to see young lives anchored in God's truth regarding the most important issues they'll face?

Even with that goal in mind, it's all too easy to get caught up in our day-to-day tasks and lose sight of the fact that our children are entering adolescence right under our noses. It's also tempting to allow discomfort or embarrassment to get in the way when it comes to speaking intentionally with our kids about how their bodies are changing, what pressures and temptations they might face in the coming years, and how they can remain true to God's calling even during the turbulent teen years.

Through the counsel set forth in this book, Robin places a loving arm around your shoulders and shows you how to chart a course that will lead to fruitful, uplifting talks and memories that both you and your daughter will treasure for years to come. She presents a beautiful vision to mothers who want to have crucial and relationship-building conversations with their daughters as they embark on the journey toward womanhood. What's more, she reminds her readers that just as every girl is unique, so is every mom—and that's perfectly okay!

Focus on the Family has counted it a privilege to partner with Robin over the years by publishing her Christy Miller and Sierra Jensen series—and now the book you hold in your hands. In fact, *Before Your Tween Daughter Becomes a Woman* should hit shelves nearly thirty-five years to the day after the debut of the very first Christy Miller novel! For three-and-a-half decades Robin has impacted the hearts and lives of young readers with inspiring spiritual and moral lessons from her fictional characters. Now she's coming alongside moms (some of whom devoured her novels during their own childhoods!) with wisdom and encouragement as they steer their daughters toward godly adulthood.

So take a deep breath, pull up a comfortable chair, and enjoy Robin's down-to-earth advice, practical tips, and heartwarming anecdotes. I'm confident you and your daughter will reap benefits that will pay eternal dividends!

Jim Daly
PRESIDENT, FOCUS ON THE FAMILY

a note from
my grown daughter

When my own mother, Robin, asked me to write this note, I realized that I am always asking, "How do I do this?" Like many of my friends, I search for relevant information on mommy forums. I call on my mom friends, and I scour social media posts aimed at moms like me.

Guiding a tween daughter into womanhood is one of the hardest "How do I do this?" questions. "How do I explain to my daughter the ways that her body will soon be changing?"

Most of all, I love looking to God's Word when it comes to answering these heart cries of motherhood. One of my favorite examples of preparing a woman for a pivotal moment in her life occurs in the book of Esther:

> Before a young woman's turn came to go in to King Xerxes, she had to complete twelve months of beauty treatments prescribed for the women, six months with

oil of myrrh and six with perfumes and cosmetics. And this is how she would go to the king: Anything she wanted was given her to take with her from the harem to the king's palace.

ESTHER 2:12-13

As we think about this topic, it's good to remember that no two women are exactly the same. Think about your mom friends who have different parenting styles, beauty routines, and lifestyles. Their individual lives are "prescribed" for them, and each of them is different. Indeed, this book allows you to see different options and read a variety of examples about how *you* might guide *your* daughter into womanhood. There is no one right answer.

Mothers are masters of gleaning. By taking in various words of advice, scanning online forums, and then pouring out our own hearts, we come up with what seems right and good.

When I was in fifth grade, I experienced my own "Esther moment." I put on my best dress and entered our family's living room feeling like I was one of the many princesses I had watched float down grand staircases on television and in films.

I understood that this was not a Taco Tuesday or Bible study night. This event was for me alone. My mother had made the house feel special with candles and music. The next hour was filled with yummy food, delicately clear conversation, and even spa-like treatments.

By the end of the evening, I was filled with innocent wonder and excitement regarding my next chapter, my entry into womanhood. My mother had given me the tools I needed to be prepared for that moment that comes each month, but there was so much more to our time together: My mom opened a door for me that, for previous generations, had been locked tight. We *celebrated* me becoming a woman rather than viewing the transition as some dark secret that was taboo to even mention.

That special evening changed me forever. My mother became someone I could trust with my secrets on an even deeper level. Before that time, I had kept quiet about many of life's questions instead of opening up and sharing my heart. But now I knew that my mother would listen before she spoke and that her arms were always open to me.

Looking back now, I see how much that time taught me about God. How He wants me to share my heart. How He wants me to celebrate who He created me to be, rather than feeling confused or even ashamed about myself. How He wants me to value His wisdom over my own.

As women, we have a deep desire to celebrate each other. Graduations, bridal parties, bachelorette parties, and baby showers bring us together to celebrate big moments and ring in new seasons. In the years since that evening with my mom, I have leaned on my experience of being celebrated into womanhood to help other young girls celebrate their womanhood. I believe that welcoming a tween into womanhood deserves the same level of preparation and excitement as any new season on the horizon.

With that in mind, I invite you to dive into this book and explore how you might celebrate your daughter's entrance into a pivotal season. I suggest that you take a few deep, cleansing breaths first. Prepare your heart for all the questions that might arise. Prepare yourself for the tears of possible pain from your past, and for the tears of joy that come with changing a young woman's future for the better.

May you be filled with pure excitement as you celebrate with your daughter her journey into womanhood.

Rachel Schwartz

"a daughter's wish"

Come to me when my heart is young

I want you, Mom, to be the one

Who reveals the mysteries

Of what is to come

When my heart is still young.

ROBIN JONES GUNN

hello, beautiful reader

All the signs are there, aren't they? Your daughter is changing, and each day seems to propel her closer to puberty. How did she grow up so quickly?

You want this change to be a positive experience for her. You want her to feel good about herself and her body. But how can you do that? How can you speak wisdom and encouragement into her life when all she wants to do is be alone in her room?

I see you. I know what you're feeling. I applaud you for being intentional about entering into this new season of her life and seeking ways to make it a good experience.

This book will help you to create significant, positive moments with your daughter. You'll find ideas on how to connect with her in ways that will profoundly deepen your relationship and bond the two of you together in the years ahead.

This is your chance to make a sacred fuss over her.

Don't pull back. It doesn't matter how you ended up in the role of "mom" in her life, whether by birth or another happy blessing. The undeniable fact is that you are the most important voice in her coming-of-age story. Even if your input seems unwanted right now, what she will remember years from now is that you cared enough to make this milestone comfortable and affirming for her.

You can do this. You really can.

Why I Care

When my daughter was maturing, I asked friends for ideas on how they marked their own daughters' journeys into womanhood. A few of them shared personal stories about how things had played out with their own daughters, but only a few had suggestions on how to enter this season in a positive way.

I was determined to celebrate the change. So, knowing how much my little girl loved tea parties, music, and dance, I planned a Welcome to Womanhood party for Rachel. Simple, sweet, cozy, and intimate. Just what she liked. The party was a success, and soon other moms asked me what I'd done. I was invited to discuss the subject at women's events and on radio programs. I even wrote a gift book titled *Gentle Passages: Guiding Your Daughter into Womanhood*.

That book eventually went out of print, but the requests kept coming from moms of preteen girls. They wanted an updated book that gave more direction and advice. Many of the young moms who wrote to me had grown up reading my

Christy Miller novels and were looking for mentoring advice now that their daughters were entering their teen years.

I knew I needed to write a new book. This book. So I brought up the topic on social media. The flood of responses surprised me. I heard from women all over the world. Some of the stories brought me to tears due to the pain of those women's journeys into adolescence. Others made me smile at their creativity. I've drawn from and combined excerpts of those responses in the "Dear Robin . . ." sections at the end of each chapter.

I also discovered something interesting about you, dear mothers everywhere. I learned that as you watch your daughter enter the springtime of her life, you're aware that you are also moving further along into the summer of your days. Certain patterns have been established. Certain relationships haven't changed. Old hurts sometimes bubble to the surface. Complicated feelings rise in you along with the elevated hormones in your daughter.

Why do some things about her suddenly bother you so much? How did the interactions between you become so messy? What happened to the sweet and silly girl who used to make you laugh? Why is she now glaring at you, and why do you want to say things to her that you never imagined would come out of your mouth?

Both of you are changing. At the same time.

Physically, emotionally, mentally, spiritually—it's a tsunami of change. Premenopausal meets preadolescence is no joke.

That's why I've included some chapters in this book specifically for you, focused on what you need as you head into this next season as a woman and a mother. I knew it wasn't enough to write a book that simply tossed a bunch of creative projects at you. The idea wasn't to give you lots of new pictures to post on social media. I wanted to help you prepare for the next season in ways that are life-giving for you, as well as for your daughter. When you are at your best, when your heart is full and at peace, you will have an abundance of everything you need to give to your daughter.

A Sacred Celebration

Giving out of abundance is much different from going through the motions of "the talk" just so you can check this foreboding task off the list and be able to say that you did what was expected of you.

You are initiating one of many valuable conversations with your daughter. You are building a bridge that the two of you can use many times in the years ahead to journey back and forth into each other's lives. Gaining access to her heart and opening yours to her starts now.

You are not having "the talk." You are starting a conversation.

I hope you understand that *Before Your Tween Daughter Becomes a Woman* is not designed to be handed to a young girl. This book is for *you*—the mom or stepmom, the dad, the mentor, the sister, the aunt, or the grandmother—to equip you to be proactive in a young girl's life and to instill in her coming-of-age transition a sense of the sacred as well as the celebration.

4

Have you ever noticed that it's nearly impossible to separate a daughter from her mother? No matter what your relationship is like, no matter how many issues or miles or other people come between the two of you in the years ahead, an invisible thread will always connect you. If you have the mom role in a young girl's life, it's critical for you to be present and tuned in so she knows that you want to bond with her.

Your daughter might be an early blossoming girl, or she might be a late bloomer. Watch for the signs. Are her emotions becoming more elevated—more quickly and intensely expressed? Is the pigmented area around her nipples beginning to enlarge? Is she experiencing a growth spurt or sprouting sparse pubic hair? Does she need to start using deodorant and do a better job of washing her face?

We've all heard that girls are physically maturing earlier with each generation. That's why I chose to initiate the important conversations with my daughter as soon as some of these physical indicators appeared. She was almost ten years old, and I didn't want to stall or wait too long. I didn't want to somehow miss the golden opportunity to be the first one in her young life to address these unavoidable topics. More than that, I wanted to plan a special celebration that would speak to her in her love language.

My daughter, Rachel, whose note appeared at the beginning of the book, is now married with children of her own. Our close relationship is one of my most treasured gifts. We've both had to work on our communication, and we've both had plenty of do-overs. Grace upon grace has brought us to where we are today, and I'm so grateful. I asked Rachel for her input on this book, and what she suggested was golden. She added touches of beauty, just as she does in all areas of her life.

Rachel and I both look back and see that her Welcome to Womanhood party helped establish a structure and pattern for our relationship that was far more valuable than either of us realized at the time. That was the day when we laid the foundation for the friendship we both cherish today.

I believe that you can have the same bridge-building experience.

All Moms Are Included

I want you to know that even if your own childhood was bumpy, this book can help equip you now. If your relationship with your daughter isn't all you dreamed it would be, this book can help change its trajectory. And if you already have a good relationship with your daughter, you can still improve it by making this transition time in her life a lovely and *honoring* experience.

Before Your Tween Daughter Becomes a Woman will undoubtedly find its way into the hands of many moms, stepmoms, grandmas, aunts, sisters, mentors, counselors, and even some dads. Please know that I am including all of you when the term *mom* appears on these pages. And think of the "daughter" referred to throughout the book as any young girl who has been entrusted to you. Your role as the mother figure in her life, regardless of how you came into that position, gives you the opportunity to serve as one of the clearest, truest, most loving voices in her life. She needs to be able to trust you rather than look anywhere else for the wisdom she needs and longs to hear.

Other sources can offer input and provide details about how her body will soon change. Some already have. Many voices—the internet, books, teachers, and even her peers—will provide information. But will any of them speak the powerful words of affirmation that she desperately needs? Will any of them celebrate her? Will any of them elevate and honor her? Likely not. *That* privilege lies with you.

You are the one who can best bring a sense of the sacred to this natural passage from childhood to womanhood.

And I'm excited to show you how.

Dear Robin . . .
When you asked what our experience was like when
we were about to enter puberty, I started crying at the
memory. My first period came when I was at school, and
it showed on my jeans. Some of the girls made fun of me,
but one of them said she'd go with me to the nurse's office.
I didn't know what was happening, but the nurse said it
was normal and that I shouldn't be afraid.

The nurse gave me some pads and a booklet. She told
me to talk to my mother when I got home. The problem
was that I lived with my dad, and when I told him, he
didn't know what to do. He gave me some money and
drove me to the store. While he waited in the car, I walked
down the aisle and tried to figure out which box I needed.
I was shaking when I went through the checkout line and
thought everyone was staring at me.

My daughter is only five, but I am determined to

make things easier for her. I would love for you to help me understand how it can be a positive experience—or even, as you said, a chance to create a celebration for her. Thank you for helping us young moms do it differently for our girls.

Start Now

What are some ways you might put the ideas from this chapter into action? What portions of the chapter stood out to you? Here are some possible points of action:

- Make a note of any subtle changes you see in your daughter's body, and watch for more.
- Talk to her father about what's to come and get him on board with how you want this transition to be a positive experience.
- If you're a stepmother, sister, aunt, grandmother, or other influential woman, evaluate if you should talk to the other mom/women in the life of your tween girl so that you can all be united. She will appreciate the combined affirmation.

Notes

_____

_____

_____

_____

_____

heart to heart

Do you believe every young girl needs to know that she is intricately and wonderfully created by God? Do you agree that being female is a beautiful, complicated mystery, and that your daughter is a one-of-a-kind woman who has a future brimming with possibilities?

Good.

That means you and I share the same beliefs. That's important because this book focuses on how you can best communicate those foundational truths to your daughter. Your voice, your smile, your clear eyes—they should always feel like home to her. You want her to believe that you see her and desire to know her.

You Are Her Safe Haven

It's amazing to think of being your daughter's haven, isn't it? You are a destination. For the rest of her life, she can come to you. You want her to know that you are the safest person and a consistent refuge in her life. You can build a relationship between the two of you in which she can always be herself, feel accepted, and settle in at any time for meaningful conversation.

The way she views her body, her personality, her appearance, and her abilities—as well as her weaknesses—will radically affect her for the rest of her life. She is in many ways at her most vulnerable during the time between childhood and adulthood. Her tender heart is most open to both truth and lies.

Your words hold great power with your daughter, even if she seems to roll her eyes at everything you say. The truths and affirmations you speak will settle in her heart and remain with her throughout her life. Both positive and negative comments—even ones she simply overhears—can grow deep roots during adolescence. This is why you must choose your words wisely.

Be the truthteller in her life.

One year at summer camp I heard a boy say that I had "knobby knees." I went back to my cabin, put on my only pair of jeans, and wore them the rest of the week, even though the weather was hot. It was a long time before I wore shorts again in public. My grandma was the one who noticed. She asked what happened to my cute shorts, and I told her that I had knobby knees. Notice I didn't say that *someone told me* I had knobby knees. In my mind, the words had become truth.

"Not so," said my grandma. "I've seen knobby knees, and I've seen your knees. Yours are not knobby. Be kind to your knees. They still move without causing pain. Why not let your healthy legs wear shorts if they want to?"

That's all it took for me to open my shorts drawer again. Her words blasted the criticism right off of my stuck-on-repeat thoughts. Looking at old photos, I can see now that I did have somewhat knobby-*ish* knees back when I was one of the tallest girls in my sixth-grade class. But that imperfect physical feature went from being a catastrophe to a mild annoyance because a dear woman in my life urged me to be kind to my knees.

So watch for small changes in your daughter's behavior. Did she stop wearing her hair in a ponytail? Maybe someone made a comment about her ears. Has she changed what she eats or the amount she eats? She may have internalized someone's comment about her weight.

This is when you can use your mom superpowers to counteract the comments that have embedded themselves in her thoughts. Share with her a hurtful comment that you held on to when you were her age. Tell her how you shook it off, or how you accepted the opinion but didn't let it determine how you acted, what you ate, or how you dressed. Then ask if she's ever been hurt by something someone said about her. Listen carefully and calmly, then make sure she has an opportunity to express how she feels. This is your chance to dispel any lies and figure out a solution to any solvable issues.

I know a tween who became obsessed with a small mole on her cheek. She kept asking when she could start wearing makeup, and her mother realized that was because she wanted to cover the mole. At her daughter's next physical, the mom asked the doctor how to tell when a mole needed to be removed. He examined it closely and said, "I can remove it right now, if you'd like."

The daughter left the doctor's office that day with four tiny stitches on her cheek and a big smile. That small change made a huge difference in her self-image.

The daughter in your life is listening to you and learning from the way you talk about your body, your relationships, and your feelings. What are the messages you're sending her way? This would be a great time in your life to start being kind to your knees or any other part of your body. Show her by your words and actions that even though we all have something about us we'd change if we could, it's good and healthy to embrace how God made us and to work with that feature.

When you initiate the conversations, that gives your daughter the freedom to open up about what she's thinking and feeling. Once again you become the safe haven she can go to as she grows older.

Take the time to listen with grace and peace so that she will feel safe. Spending more one-on-one time with her might seem like a challenge and an extra demand during your busy days. There might be friction between the two of you that makes you feel more anger than empathy. In all honesty, those were the times during my parenting years when I had to pray for wisdom and direction. And I can assure you that every time I prayed, the Lord gave me exactly what I needed to take the next step in my relationship with my daughter.

God Is Your Haven

It's also comforting to know that God is always with us as parents. He is our haven. We can go to Him at any time and talk to Him about any thing.

No matter how inadequate you feel in your role as her mother, your daughter has been entrusted to you. God created her and brought her into your life. Believe it. Be thankful for it. God knew what He was doing when He gave her to you, whether that was through birth, marriage, adoption, or a mentoring relationship. She came into your life, and you can be her most influential and important mentor, influencer, and friend as the years go on.

Have you ever actually accepted those roles in your daughter's life? I remember the first time I came across Isaiah 8:18: "Here am I, and the children the LORD has given me . . ." Those words—"the LORD has given me"—seemed to echo in my head. I paused and thanked God for the two children He had given me. My prayer that day was an act of acceptance and resolution. I was thinking, *God, I have no idea what I'm doing as a mother, but here I am, humbled and openhearted to You. These are the children, the son and daughter, that You've given me. I receive them as gifts from You.*

The simple act of accepting the role I was already in as a mother allowed me to relinquish whatever control I thought I had and step into a place of confidence, believing that God was in control. God gave these children to my husband and me. He loved them and cared about their lives far more than we ever could.

Do you believe that? It's a good place to start—or, in some cases, to hit restart. Remind yourself that God is your haven. You can run to Him at any time. He sees your heart. He knows your strengths and your inadequacies. You have never been alone in your role as a mom, and you're not alone now.

Mama Trauma

I hope you had, and still have, an affirming and nurturing relationship with your mother. If you did, some of the suggestions in this book might seem like second nature to you.

However, not all of us grew up with a strong connection to our moms. Many of us look back and see that we were not nurtured or instructed in ways that instilled confidence or freedom in us. Instead, we grew up under the shadow of insecurity and shame.

If that's where you're coming from, you are not alone. Most women who shared with me details about their growing-up years said that when they went through puberty, the experience was a negative one. Some said it was traumatic and had a damaging effect on how they viewed their body and/or how they saw their mother's role in their life.

As a result, many are now at a loss regarding how to do things differently with their own daughters. This is some of what they told me:

- I don't know what to say to my daughter.
- She already knows the basics. Isn't that enough?
- I don't want to embarrass her.

- I'm worried she'll ask questions I won't want to answer or won't know how to answer.
- I think she already knows that she can come to me if she has questions.
- She's still so young. I don't want to spoil her innocence.
- I can't see how her starting her first period is something to celebrate.

Can you relate to any of these comments? I get it. "Mama trauma" is real.

Now's the time to take a deep breath. Say a little prayer. Let your mindset shift toward the possibility of fresh beginnings.

The Why

At the moment, it probably seems like being her mama was easier when she was little. Back then she relied on you for almost everything. Your motherly instincts were on high alert beginning the day she was born, and you knew how to provide food, warmth, protection, assistance, kindness, understanding, direction, and—most of all—love. All the cuteness and smiles she gave back helped you feel confident that you were doing a good job.

Now she's changing, and you find it much more challenging to provide just the right amount of direction and information along with the necessary doses of affirmation.

What are some rites of passage, besides birthdays, that you will most likely celebrate during her first twenty years? There's her high school graduation and, well, not much else. Some family and friends might offer up a cheer when she gets her driver's license, when she is accepted by her desired university, or when she is hired for that job she wanted. But do any of those moments reflect a true transition from childhood to adulthood?

Not really. Not the way that a young girl's menarche moves her from one side of childhood to the other side. *Menarche* comes from the Greek word for "beginning" and refers to a girl's first period. This event occurs for every woman in every corner of the world and has since the beginning of time. It is healthy, normal, and natural. Yet it also largely remains shrouded in silence in Western culture.

In most families it falls to the parents, particularly the mother, to address a daughter's menarche. That's why you want to be the one who initiates this important, confidence-building, and necessary conversation with your daughter.

I know mothers who proactively launched the conversation and planned something special to make this time of change memorable. I also know moms who relinquished their position when they approached this crossroads and let others serve as the more influential voices in their daughters' lives.

The moms who engaged with their daughters, no matter how awkwardly or ill-prepared, all told me that they're glad they did. For some, it took a new kind of courage, and I applaud them for being brave and creative. Many found it wasn't as daunting as they had imagined.

As for the moms who told me they missed the moment, I

Life doesn't come with a manual. It comes with a mother.

wish you could see their faces. Some are still frustrated and discouraged. Most of them said they simply put it off and waited too long. They didn't set aside the time for a vital conversation. Many said they were too paralyzed by the shame of their own past to see how they might make their daughter's experience both different and better than theirs. Those moms lowered their eyes and said, "I wish I could go back to that time in my daughter's life and do things differently."

If you're one of those moms, take heart. It's not too late. You can and should do something special *now*. Initiate a celebration. Start a new conversation. It's okay to tell your daughter you wish you'd done something sooner. Don't dwell on the past. Instead, focus on establishing a new foundation for future conversations.

It's never too late to do something meaningful—something that says to your daughter, "I see you. I love you. I want to affirm you as a woman."

Your Responsibility

When I started writing this book, I lived in Hawaii. One of the words often used in conversation on the Hawaiian island of Maui is *kuleana*. The simple meaning in English is "responsibility."

Like most Hawaiian words, *kuleana* has more than a singular meaning. It has several layers, in fact. Kuleana begins when people recognize the value of whatever gifts or talents they have to offer. Next, those people make a choice to be generous and openly give what they have because they understand it will benefit others. They are willing to be held accountable for the responsibility—the kuleana—they have taken on. It becomes a reciprocal relationship between the giver and the receiver. Both gain and are blessed because it's done in love.

That's a very different motivation than when you view responsibilities solely as obligations, when you grit your teeth while doing what you must, just to see it through.

As a mom, your kuleana with your daughter is to first recognize your worth and the valuable role you play in your relationship. Understand that what you have to offer is invaluable, then choose to generously give what you have as an act of love— an act that will benefit both of you.

"Her value is more precious than jewels and her worth is far above rubies or pearls."

Proverbs 31:10, AMP

Sharing and celebrating the mysteries of womanhood with your daughter should be a gift from the heart, not merely a chore that you're stuck with because you are her mother.

I hope you see your worth. I hope you feel motivated to take on your kuleana with much love.

Dear Robin . . .
You asked how my mom made the transition into puberty a fun mom/daughter bonding time for us. First I should say that my mom had a way of adding fun to everything. When I started to "blossom," as she called it, she took my sister and me on a surprise shopping trip to a high-end retail store. We had an appointment with a personal stylist who put us in a large, fancy dressing room. She measured us for our accurate bra sizes even though my sister didn't need one yet. Then

she brought out a bunch of bras and bathing suits for us to try on. We had so much fun! I think that since it was such a posh setup and we were all doing it together, I didn't feel any sense of embarrassment. I loved being included with my mom in such a womanly, grown-up way.

One of the best things that happened was that the stylist kept saying that I had an "elegant long torso." I was eleven, and if you'd asked me to describe my figure, I would have said I was too tall, had big feet, and my rear end was abnormally flat. I knew how I compared to other girls my age, and to be honest, I'd never felt pretty until that day. Our stylist was sophisticated and beautiful. She made it seem as if my straight, long torso was an enviable feature.

I was different when I came home that day wearing my first bra. I felt feminine and lovely. It was as if I'd been initiated into a special club and somehow my "elegant long torso" helped me qualify as an above-average young lady.

Start Now

What are some ways you might put the ideas from this chapter into action? What portions of the chapter stood out to you? Here are some possible points of action:

- Pause right now to thank God for the children He has given you.
- Embrace your kuleana and accept your role in your daughter's life.
- Determine that you *will* do something special to usher your daughter into womanhood.

- Decide how and when you are going to initiate your first "now that you're growing up" conversation.
- Ask other moms what they did when their daughters made this transition.
- Create a list of ideas gleaned from those other women and add to it some of the ideas in this book.

Notes

before your tween daughter becomes a woman

learn her language

Have you ever noticed how your children can be just like you in many ways and at the same time completely different? Your daughter is not a "mini-me." She is not simply a smaller clone who needs to be taught how to become more like you. Our children are uniquely crafted individuals who are of immense value just the way God made them.

I have often wondered if a hint of that truth isn't embedded in Proverbs 22:6: "Train up a child in the way he should go, even when he grows older he will not abandon it" (NASB). The specific wording—"the way he should go"—seems to point to a child's unique makeup with an emphasis on the child becoming fully who God created him or her to be. It *doesn't* say, "Train up a child in the way you went" or "in the opposite of the way you went."

Life has changed significantly since you were your daughter's age. Information about anything and everything is readily available with just a few taps. There is no shortage of free advice.

The responsibility for training up our children in the way they should go is on us as parents. Yet I see in this verse an emphasis on understanding exactly *who* our children are and *what* is essential for them to fulfill their place in the world. That's why it's valuable to find ways to speak directly to your daughter's heart, so that *your* voice can rise above the cacophony of other voices that come at her daily. *You* can reach your daughter in a way that no other person or device can.

So how do you begin? By learning her language.

Great concept, right? But how does a mom learn her daughter's language? I have a few suggestions:

- Become a keen observer.
- Ask nonthreatening questions.
- Pay attention to her answers as well as the hints that point to her deeper thoughts.
- Observe her expressions and body language.
- Finally, remember what you heard and observed.

Use your best motherly detective skills to pick up on the little clues. Pause to listen, and ask questions so you can uncover the keys to the mystery that is your child. Be willing to adjust your personal expectations and discover what forms of communication have the most value to your daughter.

Speaking your daughter's language means you take the time

to tune in to her world. It also communicates that you want to spend time with her because you value what she thinks and feels and has to say. You respect the things that are important to her.

The Listening Language

When my kids were teenagers, I stumbled into learning what I called the Listening Language. I found that when our son and daughter came home from school, they didn't want twenty questions. On days when they did have something to share, they would start to tell me about it. But without realizing it, I kept squelching the moment. I did this by interrupting, asking too many questions, and jumping in with advice they never asked for.

I caught myself doing this one day and determined that the next time they wanted to talk, I'd keep quiet. I'd pay attention. I'd make it clear that I was listening.

When our son came home one day and talked about something surprising that had happened in his American Sign Language class, I implemented my plan. The only sounds that came from my lips were delivered with calmness, and they mainly consisted of signs that I was paying attention. Here's the nearly complete vocabulary of the Listening Language I used that day:

- "Hmmm."
- "Oh."
- "Mm-hmm."
- "I see."
- "Wow."

- "Really?"
- "Uh-huh."

Another key to the Listening Language is that your body language should coincide with your words. Focus on relaxed posture, eye contact, understanding smiles, and eyebrows that rise or fall in sync with what you're hearing. It's a symphony of communication as you and your child are the only instruments performing this special song. Your role, at least at the start, is to provide the subtle background accompaniment that gives the music structure and foundation yet doesn't overshadow the primary theme.

The golden moment comes when your kids wrap up their purge of the situation, having received only Listening Language sounds and expressions from you. That's when they relax slightly and extend an invitation for you to speak into the moment. Maybe they're just being polite, but if they ask for your thoughts, it's likely that they sincerely want to hear what you have to say.

Be prepared to respond in a way that keeps the communication going. Refrain from saying what you've been dying to blurt out from the beginning. Instead, help your children give themselves their own best advice by asking these three questions:

1. How do you feel about all that?
2. What do you think should happen next?
3. What are you going to do?

These simple questions can lead to some of the deepest, most complex conversations you'll have with your daughter, especially as she develops both her logic and communication skills. By using Listening Language during her waterfall of expression, you just might earn the chance to take the topic deeper. I think you'll find that those three questions will keep the exchange going rather than turning the moment into an opportunity for you to command the pulpit and deliver your best sermon.

You might be surprised by how quickly the floodgates open when you ask the first question, "How do you feel about all that?" In some cases, it might be the only question you need to ask because a good cry and a warm hug could be all your daughter needs.

The second question is often the most jarring. "What do you think should happen next?" has the potential to prompt a blaring trumpet call for justice from her wounded heart: "I think she should apologize to me for what she said!" or "I think the teacher should give me an extra day to finish because my project partner was sick."

That's why the third question is vital. When you ask, "What are you going to do?" you are handing the decision-making power back to your daughter. Even if her answer is, "I want you to tell me what to do," it's a victory because she's inviting you in.

Isn't it interesting that the way to becoming the most significant voice in your daughter's world is through a conversation in which you spend most of the time keeping your lips closed? You are a filter for her, as well as an instructor, and have been since before she was born. The rhythms of your communication will change throughout the seasons of her life.

Shared Loves

When you're ready to take Listening Language from the initial "you/me" phase into the "us" phase, you'll want to find something you both like.

In our case, my daughter and I both love *Anne of Green Gables*. You, too? That's great. But even if you're not familiar with it, you'll likely understand how watching the film version together became such a shared love for us. You and your daughter might have another movie you both love, and you can add some fun to your next viewing the way we did with *Anne*.

We discovered the Sullivan Entertainment version when Rachel was in second grade. I bought the series starring Megan Follows as the title character, and my daughter and I instituted our annual "Anne with an 'E' Day" that lasted into her college years. On the last day of school each year, which was usually a half-day, I would have everything set up by the time Rachel arrived home. She and I had the TV reserved for the next six hours.

Our "Anne with an 'E' Day" was an interactive experience. When Anne and Diana did their three-legged race at the church picnic, we tied our legs together and skittered around the island in the kitchen. As Anne prepared her special tea party for Diana (who was "sampling" the raspberry cordial), we sipped cherry juice from my aunt's special crystal glasses and nibbled on small, triangular, crustless sandwiches.

We crossed our arms with Anne and closed our eyes as she boarded the borrowed rowboat and arranged her long hair to look like the Lady of Shalott. When Matthew collapsed in the field, Rachel and I always reached for the Kleenex at the same time, every time. We stood straight and tall in a show of camaraderie at the recital of "The Highwayman." Along with Anne, we chanted, "When the moon is a ghostly galleon tossed upon cloudy seas . . ."

By my estimation, we did this for at least eleven years. It became *our thing*.

One year my daughter wanted to include a friend, who came over with her mother and her sister. They didn't get it when we clomped around the kitchen island in the three-legged race. They didn't care for the cherry juice. Nor did they even make it to the scene with Anne and Gilbert on the bridge, when Rachel and I leaned our heads on each other's shoulders and swooned, "Oh, Gilbert Blythe!" It wasn't Rachel's friend's thing—nor her mother's or sister's.

It was our thing, and we never invited them or anyone else to join us again. This became one of our shared loves. Just for us.

The surprise was how some exceptionally good conversations about boys, careers, and death flowed out of our annual "Anne with an 'E' Day." Anne's stories initiated conversations about real life, and I've always been grateful for those free-flowing talks.

Take a moment now to think about something that you and your daughter both enjoy. Think about the steps you can take to make it "your thing." Your shared love. Start by considering the times when your natural interests overlap, such as baking, crafting, sports, shopping, music, or travel. Having something special for just the two of you and creating your own traditions around it will bond you in sweet and fun ways.

Promises Kept

Another aspect of learning a shared language involves making and keeping a promise to create some form of celebration when your daughter enters puberty. The trust you'll build with her through this process is more important than it might appear at first. So don't let uncertainty hamper you—go ahead and promise her something to anticipate when she reaches puberty.

For instance, has she been asking to have her ears pierced? If that's something you've already agreed to, but have been saying, "Not now, but one day . . . ," why not promise that when she starts her period, you'll take her to have her ears pierced? Make it a shared, fun experience—a "just us" moment.

Does she want to wear makeup like an older sister or a friend at school? Promise that you'll make an appointment for her with a beauty specialist. Let a professional show her the best way to care for her skin and apply age-appropriate makeup.

When you create a shared experience around wearing cosmetics, your daughter will be less likely to sneak a tube of mascara into her backpack and take lessons from other girls gathered around a mirror in the school bathroom.

Lots of moms have told me stories of their promises kept, including overnight trips to a hotel, conference, or retreat. Their daughter's love language was quality time, which meant they valued the shared time together away from the usual routine at home. If you plan a getaway and it happens to be linked to business or other commitments you have, make sure that your responsibilities don't rob the two of you of lots of free time together.

I recently spoke at a women's retreat during which a teen girl kept hanging around my book table. She wanted to talk and talk and talk to me. I finally asked if she was going to do any of the planned free-time activities, such as crafts or hikes. She replied, "I only came because my mom said we would do things together. But when we got here, she volunteered to help in the kitchen."

This teen told me that she had tried to help in the kitchen, too, but the other women had urged her to find something fun to do. Apparently, lengthy conversations with me about her softball team was the only fun thing she could find. I felt sad for her. Her mother's promise was hollow. I also felt for her mom, because the next time she suggested that the two of them have a girls' weekend, you just knew that her daughter was not going to be interested. Speaking your daughter's language means you actually take the time to tune in to her, because you value what she thinks, feels, and has to say.

Dear Robin . . .
I wanted to tell you how my mom affirmed me and established a strong female-to-female connection between us. When I was growing up, I was such a tomboy that I shopped in the men's department. I was an athlete and wanted clothes that let me move. I had no interest in

tea parties and pretty little ponies. My mom is artistic, generous, and creative, so when I turned sixteen, she gave me a pair of pearl earrings in a velvet jewelry box and said, "Every woman needs a pair of pearl earrings."

My response was, "Heeey . . . thaaanks?"

I got the impression that those earrings were my mom's way of saying, "Welcome to the Woman Club." They pointed to the other side of the tomboy years and shaped my view of what was yet to come.

Even though I didn't fit the stereotype of what femininity looked like among the other young girls of my generation, I am so glad that my mom affirmed my identity as a woman during my teen years. I wasn't confused about the way God created me because my mom made it clear that it was okay to be a strong, capable, no-frills, athletic woman. That didn't change. Yet her gift of the pearl earrings instilled a sense of a greater femininity that was yet to be awakened in my life.

My favorite part of our story is how my relationship with my mom grew closer as I grew older. When I got married, I asked my mom to be my matron of honor. And yes, of course I wore the pearls on my wedding day. Now that my husband and I have two children, I plan to continue that tradition with our daughter.

Start Now

What are some ways you might put the ideas from this chapter into action? What portions of the chapter stood out to you?

Here are some possible points of action:

- Practice using Listening Language.
- Discover your "shared love." Don't worry about how many attempts you make before something clicks for both of you.
- Arrange a special activity for just the two of you and establish it as a tradition.
- Prepare a special gift for your daughter, such as a piece of jewelry that's a family heirloom, for when she enters puberty.

Notes

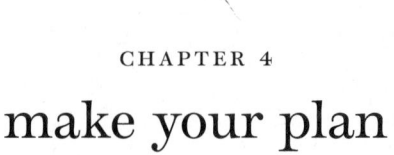

make your plan

Is your creative mind beginning to hum with ideas of what might work well with your daughter? Good! Now, let me help you make your plan.

For those of you who love checklists, this next part is just for you. Let's start with the "don'ts," then move on to the "dos."

DON'T . . .

- wait too long before you set up a special time with your daughter.
- assume others are going to do your job for you.
- think that one size fits all when it comes to what girls like.

DO . . .

- plan ahead and be intentional about setting up a special time and place.
- treat this as a celebration.
- prepare yourself and your words ahead of time.

The next question is that of what style will work best for your daughter and you. Is she a pro-fuss or no-fuss girl? Is she pro-group or no-group?

You'll find some stories about and suggestions for each of these approaches in this chapter, but first I want to emphasize that the most important ingredient of all is your full and complete attention. Whatever you do, make sure your moments are marked by eye contact, soft smiles, and unhurried words. She might not want you to hold her hand anymore, but this is your chance to assure her that you can still hold her heart.

Your daughter knows the difference between when you're merely present and when you are all there. Let her know that you only have eyes for her. You *want* to be with her. She can take all the time in the world to process the conversation and ask as many questions as she wants. No phones. No distractions. Full attention.

When you have that strategy in mind from the beginning, this conversation will be set apart from the hurried and incomplete conversations of a normal day. For moms who feel like they live in survival mode, shifting from one urgency to another, being intentional and focused during a devoted time with your tween will be a gift to her, in and of itself. I think you'll find that this time will be a gift to you as well.

Your objective for this conversation is to establish that you care deeply about your daughter, you are available to her, and—since you are already on the other side of these changes—you want to be the one who says, "Welcome to womanhood."

So what's the best way to do that? Think about your daughter's last birthday party or comments she made about a recent event or even a friend's birthday party. Does she want lots of friends to join in, or would she prefer something simple and quiet? Does she love to give gifts, receive gifts, or both? How much does she like the hoopla of decorating for Christmas or other holidays? The answers to these questions will help you determine if she's a pro-fuss or no-fuss kind of girl, or a pro-group or no-group sort of young woman.

The examples that follow will also help you clarify what your daughter prefers so that you can start putting your plan into motion with confidence.

Fuss

My daughter, Rachel, was all about the fuss and frills, but not the big groups. As I mentioned earlier, I knew the best thing I could do for her would be to set up a private party at home for just the two of us and bring out our china teacups. I set the date and made sure it was a good time for my husband and son to be out of the house. I created a very girly invitation and sealed the envelope with a heart sticker. The invitation was waiting for her on her pillow the day before the party.

Rachel was all in. While she was at school the next day, I went to a bakery and bought a four-layer mini cake topped with pink rosebuds. I prepared a gift bag for her with tissue paper fluffed out at the top. Inside was a small box of panty liners, a travel-size bottle of body spray, a miniature bar of her favorite chocolate, and a tube of watermelon-flavored lip balm.

When Rachel came home from school, she went to her room to get ready. We lived in the Pacific Northwest at the time, and the rainy weather meant we usually wore jeans and sweaters for nine months of the year. On that cold February evening I had the fire going. Mellow music floated through the house. The coffee table was set with my favorite teapot, china teacups, the yummy-looking cake, a tiny bouquet of flowers, and her gift bag. I even found sugar cubes decorated with pink flowers.

All the frills.

I heard Rachel's bedroom door open and looked up from the couch to see her at the top of the stairs wearing her favorite dress-up gown—a pale blue, flowing bridesmaid's dress I had worn at my sister's wedding. My daughter floated down the stairs with a grace all her own and sat beside me on the couch. I loved her expression as she took in the gift bag and the sweets.

"This is all for you," I said as I cut the cake. "I want to celebrate you!"

"Why?" she asked.

I poured the tea, and we stirred in the sugar cubes and cream.

"You're growing up and maturing. Before long, you'll be leaving girlhood and entering the next season of your life. I wanted to celebrate that change and, as your mother, I wanted to be the first one to personally welcome you to womanhood."

I held up my teacup, and she lifted hers. We sat together like fine ladies as I explained the ancient mystery of how her body would change and what would happen next. I gave her a clear explanation in simple terms that I knew would make sense to her. Her eyes were wide, and her heart was open even wider. I wanted her to see that she could trust me with delicate conversations. The moment felt natural to both of us.

In a hushed voice she asked, "Boys don't have anything like this happen to them every month, do they?"

"No," I told her. "Only a woman's body is designed this way. God made a woman's body to carry, nurture, and deliver new life. This was a privilege not given to men. Only to women."

"And not even to angels," Rachel added.

I paused. "That's true. Not even angels can have babies. Only women."

Her blue eyes didn't blink. "It's an honor to be a woman, then, isn't it?"

Her comment caught me off guard. I'm not sure I had ever considered my femaleness to be an honor. I felt my throat tighten as I realized that my daughter's attitude and response were completely different than my own when the realities of puberty were revealed to me. Shame would not be among the heirlooms passed down to her. (I'll tell you more about my story later.)

Rachel opened her gift bag. A casual explanation followed regarding how to best use the panty liners. I wanted her to know that she had the freedom to use them every day if it helped her feel confident and prepared. She tried out the lip balm and gave her bare arm a spritz of the strawberry-scented body spray.

At the bottom of the gift bag was a tiny box that held two coconut truffles, which brought a smile to her face. "My favorite," she said. "You remembered."

I invited her to ask me questions. She had a few. Mostly she wanted to understand both male and female organs and body parts. I hadn't expected that and wasn't quite prepared.

We went up to my bedroom, and I pulled an old biology textbook from my bookshelves. She and I cuddled up on the bed, and the conversation continued as we looked at the medical illustrations together. It felt natural to point to the various body parts and explain how a husband and wife bring their bodies together.

Going into the specifics felt more comfortable than I thought it would, and the pictures definitely helped. It's a good idea to gather whatever resource materials you might need ahead of time so you'll feel prepared for whatever conversations take place.

Rachel and I went back downstairs to the cozy setting with the fire, the remaining sweets, and the soft music. Through the front windows we saw that it had begun to snow. The fluffy snowflakes seemed to flutter in the glow of the streetlight, like tiny ivory ballerinas wearing gilded slippers.

Rachel reached for my hands and said the familiar words she had been uttering since she was a toddler. "Come on, Mom. Let's dance."

We twirled and sashayed, dipped and swayed in response to the background music, smiling at each other eye to eye, heart to heart. Neither of us will ever forget that enchanting moment.

The song ended, and to conclude our little holy hullabaloo, I placed the palm of my hand on her forehead and blessed her with a familiar nighttime blessing her father and I had spoken over both our kids since they were little:

May the Lord bless you and keep you.
May the Lord make His face shine upon you
and give you His peace.
And may you always love Jesus more than anything else.

We adapted that blessing from the ancient verses in Numbers 6:24-26. Rachel received the blessing with her eyes closed and her lips upturned with a contented smile. I leaned closer and whispered, "Welcome to womanhood, my darling girl."

Just telling you about this warms me all over again. The time was powerful, peaceful, and relationship altering for both of us. I can honestly say that up until that day, I had never thanked God for the annoyance of monthly periods. I had never felt grateful for the way my body did what it was supposed to do.

Rachel changed the way I thought about menstruation that day because she was right: It is an honor to be a woman.

No-Fuss

If you and your daughter have a no-frills way of connecting and you know she would be nauseous if you brought out a teapot and told Siri to play harp music, here's a completely different scenario for you.

A friend told me about the "It's an Honor to Be a Woman"

day she stumbled onto with her eight-year-old daughter. I think she did a great job of sailing through the moment with little fuss but lots of open doors for communication.

Here's what happened: Her daughter sidled up to her in the kitchen one afternoon and spilled a distressing bit of info she had heard on the playground. With a concerned expression, the girl asked if it was true.

My friend stopped everything, looked her innocent firstborn in the eyes, and said, "The part that's true is that your body is going to change in a few years. The part that's not true is what you heard about bleeding to death."

Her daughter looked only slightly comforted, so my friend said, "Think about all the questions you have regarding what you heard, and let's talk about it when you go to bed."

That night, when her daughter was settled in the safe familiarity of her room, my friend sat on her daughter's bed. "Before you ask your questions," this mother said, "I want to read you some verses I've always liked." She then read Psalm 139:13-14 from *The Living Bible*:

You made all the delicate, inner parts of my body and knit them together in my mother's womb. Thank you for making me so wonderfully complex! It is amazing to think about. Your workmanship is marvelous—and how well I know it.

PSALM 139:13-14

Placing her palm on her lower abdomen, my friend said, "This is where my womb is. This is where God knit you together inside of me. Since you're a girl, like me, you have a womb too. It's also called a uterus."

From there, she explained how a lining of blood builds up each month to prepare a cushioned place for a baby to grow. The body knows each month that when no baby is in there, the lining isn't needed so it slowly flows out of the woman's body.

It wasn't a lot of information, but it was enough. The fear of bleeding to death was removed. The other gruesome things she had heard at school were resolved after a few questions, and her daughter's eight-year-old imagination was satisfied and relieved that it would probably be a few years before she had her first period.

A no-fuss approach helped this mother start the conversation, and now she could keep adding details that fit with her daughter's age and ability to understand.

Of all the things my friend did, I especially like two of them: First, she stopped what she was doing and addressed her daughter's main questions directly, but also shifted the more in-depth conversation to when she knew they wouldn't be interrupted—to a time when they could keep the communication going in private. Second, I like that she started the conversation in her daughter's bedroom by reading Scripture. She brought a sense of the sacred to their time by revealing what God has to say about the human body, thus elevating the schoolyard talk to a topic that should be respected.

Group

Do you think your girl would prefer a group event that honors preteen girls? I've heard from several women who host gatherings like this. One of them called theirs a "Girls Are Amazing" party and held one each year for the fifth-grade girls at their church. (I'll share more about the details of their event in chapter 6 under the heading "Respect Demonstrated in a Group.")

At a Girls Are Amazing party, the conversation about how their bodies will change occurs in a safe environment and includes information about both spiritual and physical maturity. The moms say it's an effective way to help their daughters enter puberty and creates opportunities for additional conversations on topics such as skin care, hair, makeup, friendships, and boys.

The benefit of honoring many young girls at the same time with a special event is that there's power in combining the voices of all the mentors who speak. One of the speakers might be an expert in fashion and can demonstrate how to put together outfits that are mom-approved, work well for a young girl's changing shape, and yet still look cute and current. This can be a big help for moms who are waging an uphill battle over what their blossoming daughters want to wear.

Another speaker might share an inspirational message that incorporates truths from God's Word in a way that communicates directly to a preadolescent's heart and mind. I'm so grateful for the teachers, speakers, and mentors my daughter admired when she was growing up. They were able to say exactly what I'd been trying to communicate, but in a role-model way that helped Rachel better remember what they talked about. More than once she would repeat to me things they suggested, and I would think, *Hey, I've been saying that for years.*

Let's be honest—all moms sound like white noise to their daughters at some point. It's sad, but true. That's why we should be grateful for other women, other voices, who speak truth to our daughters in ways they can hear and take to heart. Instead of being jealous of those influential voices, let's thank God for them.

One of the bonuses of your daughter attending a gathering where many facets of growing up are discussed is that it will help her feel included. She becomes part of a special bunch— the guests of honor at a special party. Since other friends also receive the same information, this can help draw them closer as they grow up together.

One caution: Don't use such an event to check having "the talk" off your list, assuming that everything your daughter needs to know has now been covered. The purpose of these group events is to *start* the conversation. It still falls on you, the mom, to make sure that singular Welcome to Womanhood moment happens between just the two of you. Your one-on-one time together will give her a chance to ask any questions she's been pondering and give you a chance to build on the party's theme about how special women's bodies are and how to respect them.

You'll be at a disadvantage if you simply drop your daughter off at the event, pick her up when it's over, and never engage in a deeper conversation. Consider the event an invitation to enter your daughter's world and to keep the conversation going.

No-Group

If a large group event isn't a possibility or a preference for you or your daughter, then consider the no-group approach by setting up a special time for just the two of you. Or keep it small and include one close friend.

I know two moms who are longtime friends. They have daughters who are the same age, and the girls had been best friends since they were toddlers. The girls were as close as sisters. As the girls approached puberty, the moms decided to do something special together since their daughters were inseparable.

They planned a luncheon for the four of them and reserved a small, private room at a restaurant. In a lovely, grown-up way, the daughters were treated like young ladies as the moms took turns sharing the details of puberty and tag-teaming as they answered questions.

The daughters also tag-teamed with their own questions, and the conversation easily rolled into other topics, which made the time feel full and varied.

One of the best results of this approach was that the girls had each other to talk with on a deeper level, since neither of them had sisters. Sometimes a girl needs someone other than her mom to go to; the luncheon confirmed that they had another woman who cared about them and was also available during their growing-up years.

As you plan the best way to celebrate with your daughter, be kind to yourself. Don't overthink it. There's no exact right or wrong way to do this. If you have several daughters, keep in mind that your plan will vary with each of them. Don't worry about trying to be fair or equal. Focus on the individual needs of each daughter.

The objective is to try. To make an effort. To show that you care. That's the primary message you want your daughter to receive, no matter what approach you take or how "successful" your attempt turns out. This is an ongoing conversation, one you can add to at any time. Just make sure to start the conversation.

How Much Do I Explain?

When it came to how much information I was going to address in our conversation, I went by the example I read in Corrie ten Boom's biography, *The Hiding Place*. Corrie described how, when she was a young girl seated with her father on a train, she asked him about a sexual term she'd heard but didn't recognize.

> He turned to look at me, as he always did when answering a question, but to my surprise he said nothing. At last he stood up, lifted his traveling case from the rack over our head, and set it on the floor.
>
> "Will you carry it off the train, Corrie?" he said.
>
> I stood up and tugged at it. It was crammed with the watches and spare parts he had purchased that morning.
>
> "It's too heavy," I said.
>
> "Yes," he said. "And it would be a pretty poor father who would ask his little girl to carry such a load. It's the same way, Corrie, with knowledge. Some knowledge

is too heavy for children. When you are older and
stronger you can bear it. For now you must trust me
to carry it for you."

And yet, as much as this wonderful example of a loving parent
helped set a guideline for me, I also knew that if my daughter
had specific questions that I chose not to address, she had other
sources she could easily go to.

Thus my solution was to address every one of her questions,
even if my response was, "I don't know how to answer that right
now, but I will later. I want to keep talking about this with you."

Sometimes I said, "That would be a good thing for us to talk
about with Dad." I knew my husband would be able to give a
more clinical answer on some topics. The benefit of including
him was that she knew she could ask questions of both of us.

I remember one night when she and I each brought our
Bibles to the conversation. I took her to Genesis 1:27 and 5:2,
where God's original plan is clearly stated. It says He created
male and female. Just male and female.

The main thing was to not freak out over some of the terms
she'd heard or specifics she asked about. She had already been
exposed to far more than I was at her age. I could carry much
for her until she was older, but at the moment my goal was to
keep nurturing a warmth and openness between us.

Dear Robin . . .
This is a great topic because it needs to be talked about. My
mom did something thoughtful when I started my period.

She and I are a lot alike, and she knew that all I'd want to do was hide in my room. She brought me a cup of cocoa, a toasted English muffin with honey (my favorite comfort food), and a hot water bottle. Then she handed me a small stack of envelopes tied with a green polka-dotted ribbon. Once again, my favorite.

I got comfortable and opened the cards that were from the women in our large family. My mom had asked each of them to write me a private note with some advice on becoming a woman. One of my aunts, who is really beautiful, included a faded Polaroid from when she was my age. I never would have recognized her! She was gangly and had braces, and her hair was wild.

In her letter she wrote, "What you believe on the inside will soon take over the outside. I believe you are beautiful. What do you believe?"

Every letter had a similar gem. I felt as if the women in my family had crafted an invisible crown for me with all their shining words. I read their letters many times during my teen years and kept them in a special box in my closet. Each time I read them I felt as if their advice and blessings were giving me courage and renewed compassion for myself and for others.

I'm twenty-eight now, and two of the women who contributed to my mom's project have passed. That makes the gift of their words to me in their handwriting more treasured than ever.

Start Now

What are some ways you might put the ideas from this chapter into action? What portions of the chapter stood out to you?
Here are some possible points of action:

- Figure out if your daughter is a fuss or no-fuss—and a group or no-group—kind of girl.
- Brainstorm what you want to do *for* her or *with* her.
- Consider whom you'll need to partner with in order to help make it happen.
- Don't delay. Prepare in advance so that you'll have things ready when it comes time to bless her.

Notes

make your plan

celebrate the moment

Time flies. We all know that.

My question for you, dear caring mama, is what can you do to make time stop for one memorable moment? Instead of letting the wave of oncoming puberty wash over both of you with all its emotional, shore-pounding certainty, how can you take your daughter by the hand and dive in together?

Pause and think. Ask God for wisdom. From all the examples and ideas shared in the previous chapters, hold on to the pieces that resonated with you. Dream a little right now. What can you do that would make your daughter feel celebrated and special?

Bestowing Gifts

For many women, young and old, it's not really a party unless gifts are involved. They don't see how their daughter will feel celebrated unless a gift is given to mark the moment—unless a flurry of wrapping paper and expressions of surprise and delight are included.

That's how it is for the women in my novel *Becoming Us*, when the ten-year-old character of Audra has her first period. Her mom organizes a small party with the women who are the most important in Audra's life. Each woman brings a small gift with a coming-of-age meaning.

For instance, Sierra gives her an assortment of flavored lip glosses and tells Audra that every single kiss has value. That's why, Sierra says, a wise young woman saves those kisses and gives them away sparingly.

Christy gives Audra a journal and tells her how helpful it was to write out all her own thoughts and prayers when she was a teen.

At the end of this sweet, gift-giving time, Audra's mother crowns her with a wreath of flowers and tells her she is a daughter of the King of kings—and to always remember *who* she is and *whose* she is.

Yes, I created this fictional moment and this group of imaginary women. But I realized it was something more when I heard from readers who arranged the same sort of coming-of-age parties for the young women in their lives, using that scene as their model.

As encouraging as that is, I also realize that some readers are cringing as they read this because gift-giving is a challenge. I'm no expert at gift-giving, but some of the women I'm closest to are. My daughter, for example, is a superb gift-giver. So is my sister. I just don't have that mindset. If you're like me, this is where you'll need to pay special attention to your daughter's love language.

Does she light up when she receives gifts, or does quality time together turn on the conversation waterfall? Does she shower you with appreciation when you do something extra for her? If she thrives on words of affirmation, you'll want to make sure you give her plenty of praise. And if being close and cuddling is still her favorite posture with you, plan your conversation-opening moment accordingly. All these are worthwhile ideas to consider.

With my daughter, I realized at our living room tea party that the gift bag I had presented to her was more of a party favor than a true gift. When she was fourteen, we made plans together for another special tea party. This time I bought her a ring that she had pointed out many times. We went to a luxurious tearoom for our celebration. When the waiter brought over a three-tiered tray filled with sweets and savories, I put my sneaky little plan into motion.

"Why don't we pray?" I suggested.

Rachel bowed her head and closed her eyes. As I was thanking God that we could enjoy this special time together, I slipped one of the cucumber sandwiches off its petite paper doily and replaced it with the ring box.

When I said "Amen," Rachel opened her eyes, saw the box,

and started crying. Without looking inside the jewelry box, she said she just knew it was the ring she had been wanting for so long. That day, that tea party, and that gift scored very high on her list of memorable moments.

If you've been saving a piece of special jewelry to pass on to your daughter, and/or if she highly values gifts, think about how you might incorporate a "bestowing moment" into your ongoing conversations. If she's still too young to care for an expensive piece of jewelry, you can still show it to her, tell her the story behind it, and promise that it will be hers one day. You'll just keep it safe for her until she's a little older.

The objective is to do whatever makes her feel adorned and adored. When messages of beauty and bestowing are communicated by a mother through gifts, it affirms to her daughter that she is of great value and highly cherished. To withhold such favor until she has "earned" the right communicates a different message—whether you intend it or not, you are communicating that she must always try to be "good enough" before she's rewarded.

Make sure your daughter receives value statements at home so she won't seek affirmation of her worth from sources that might betray her.

Try to remember what you felt at her age. How important was it for you to receive gifts, words, hugs, attention, or acts of kindness? Which of those can you give to your daughter? While you're at it, why not be extravagant about it?

The heart of a preadolescent girl is a treasure chest. She is busy collecting all that she deems important and keeping it locked in that treasure chest for safekeeping. The trouble with making hormone-induced decisions while she's out gathering gems is that not everything she holds on to is truly valuable. For instance, she likely holds on to what others say about her, how they treat her, and how they react when she enters a room or speaks up.

Do you see the potential power you wield? Your words, actions, and expressions can and should help fill the vast openness of her heart. Her heart will gravitate to the voices that tell her she's important, smart, pretty, or whatever qualities she admires most in others and wants to attain.

Let your voice be the first and the most convincing one to help her feel loved and valued. Help her learn how to discern between genuine gold and fool's gold.

Other Options

Does your daughter save her birthday cards? Does she read carefully what friends and loved ones write on those cards? This is an ideal opportunity to have her grandmas, aunts, and close adult friends send her cards that include encouragement and womanly advice. Let these special people in your daughter's life know that, when the day comes for your special celebration, you will deliver all the unopened missives to your daughter and remind her that these notes are from her women—her circle of ongoing support as she grows up.

Another way to mark the moment is to connect her

coming-of-age season with something that's of special importance to her. Did you tell her she has to wait until she's older before she can do something special, like take singing lessons? Has she been asking to get her eyebrows shaped? At what age will she start shaving her legs? When is it time for her first bra?

Any of these pivotal moments can be turned into a small celebration. You bring the joy. You get to fancy up the experience and help reduce any insecurity or embarrassment. With each small step forward, you are telling your daughter, "I'm here for you. I want to make fun memories with you."

Of course, you might hit some bumps in the road if she suggests something unexpected, like multiple piercings. One twelve-year-old told her mom that all she wanted was plastic surgery and a tattoo. She knew girls her age who had both.

If that happens, don't freak out. Just keep the conversation going. Don't dismiss her feelings behind the request. Listen to her reasons and, if necessary, press pause on the request so that you can hold the line where needed and determine the best way to explain your final decision.

A Shared Journal

If your daughter is particularly shy and only comfortable when she's free to be her introverted self, then consider sharing a journal. This is a great way to start a written conversation between the two of you. You can write a short paragraph or two on the first page of the journal, letting your daughter know that you love her. Invite her to write you back in the journal and let her know that this communication is just between the two of you. Your shared journal is a safe place for her to ask questions, make comments, draw pictures—whatever she wants to share with you.

Make it a "just between us" experience. Put the journal under each other's pillows when you write something new so that it feels like you're exchanging secret notes. Write sweet things like "I saw the way you helped your brother tie his shoes today, and I loved the way you were so kind to him. You are an incredibly good sister."

As your conversations become more comfortable, add specific notes about how her body is changing. Write something like "I bought some new body wash for you. It's in your bathroom. Let me know how you like it."

A day or two later, casually ask, "How did you like the new soap?" This might lead to a bit more explanation about how, as she's growing older, she'll be using new products to keep her body fresh. Baby steps. Prep for what is to come.

A Book for Both of You

Are you and your girl among the many mothers and daughters who enjoy reading books together? It's a great way to create a shared experience, and you can also use the book's content as a springboard for important conversations.

In my research for this book, I read a lot of nonfiction titles written for preadolescent girls, books that were designed to explain body changes. While I liked parts of almost all of them, I didn't find one that I felt comfortable endorsing or listing as a resource in this book.

That said, I still encourage you to check out the many different books available for young girls and decide if some might work well for you. I recommend that you read the book first, taking notes on the specifics you would like to talk about with your daughter.

You might want to write your thoughts in the margins or make a list of key points. That way, if you come to parts where you aren't in agreement with the author, you can be prepared to go further than the book does or provide your daughter with more or different information.

If you do give a book to your daughter, do so after your Welcome to Womanhood moment with her. Make sure she knows that you want to keep talking about it with her. That could be through your shared journal, notes in the margins of the book, or more conversation.

One of the best resources I've found for teen girls is Focus on the Family's *Brio* magazine. Many girls prefer a magazine instead of a book, and you can feel confident that the content in *Brio* will be God honoring. Plus you can use the article topics each month as a springboard for a good chat.

Include Her

Our busy lives mean that family members orbit in their own universes that rarely overlap. Is that why "Bring Your Child to Work" days and "Invite Your Parents to School" days were created? Did we actually need special occasions to help us enter each other's worlds? Maybe so.

How are things in your busy life these days? Can you think

of ways to easily include your daughter? Is there something you do on a regular basis that she wants to hear about or be included in?

I have a realtor friend who discovered that her daughter made for an adorable hostess on open house days. No one could resist her smile when she pointed them to a plate of cookies on the counter next to the flyers and her mother's business cards.

Another friend of mine who travels occasionally for her job made the effort to bring her daughter along to a business event. Those three days became a turning point in their relationship.

One mom told me that her daughter was constantly underfoot when she was trying to prepare dinner. She finally handed her daughter an apron, and their unplanned cooking lessons began. By the time the daughter was eleven, she eagerly prepared nearly all the family meals, and her favorite birthday gifts were cookbooks. By the age of twenty-four, she was an established chef who, by the way, had far surpassed her mom's cooking skills.

Try inviting your daughter to join you when it makes sense, and use the experience to share your life with her as well as nurture the friendship part of your relationship.

Dear Robin . . .
I wish more writers like you were writing books about this season of life. When my daughter was nine, I read that as a mom I should never interfere with her journey of self-discovery by imposing anything on her, because it would undoubtedly come with my own bias. The message was

that my preadolescent daughter would become stronger and more independent if I only made informational material available and then stepped away so she could develop her own problem-solving skills. She would thereby experience the empowering sense of self-sufficiency.

That made sense to me, so I bought a book about puberty and planned to leave it in my daughter's room. When I told a friend what I was doing, she said, "When she was a baby and you knew she needed to be fed, did you ever once consider dropping a bottle in her crib and closing the door so she could develop her problem-solving skills and figure out how to feed herself?"

Our conversation became intense, but in the end, my friend helped me realize that, when my daughter was a baby, she needed all of me—my closeness, my voice, my expressions, my touch. She didn't need only the nourishment I put within her reach. That's still true at this next stage of her life. She needs more than a book on her nightstand.

I changed my plan and made dinner reservations for the two of us. I'm a single mom, so my daughter knew that getting dressed up and going to a nice restaurant twenty miles away was a big deal. I was nervous and afraid of how my daughter would react, but it went great.

During dinner I told her three things I liked about her, and I said that I knew God loved her and had His hand on her life. She cried, but then she's been doing that a lot lately.

On the drive home she said she was embarrassed that

she cried. I told her it was her hormones and that they are a good thing, because they help a young girl's body change. She said she had been using my deodorant and asked if she could get her own. We had a great conversation and stayed in the car to talk for almost an hour after we arrived home.

I told her about the book I had bought for her, and she asked if we could read it together. It went great, and we've had several important and helpful conversations since then. That night was a turning point in our relationship, and I'm so glad I made the effort to do something special, even though I was nervous and felt inadequate.

Start Now

What are some ways you might put the ideas from this chapter into action? What portions of the chapter stood out to you?

Here are some possible points of action:

- Determine if your daughter responds best to words, gifts, or time together. Think about how you can create a memorable moment of celebration.
- Don't wait to purchase or prepare a gift if you've determined that's best for your girl.
- Consider getting a journal to use as a conversational tool between the two of you.
- Ask your daughter to pick out a book for you to read together and discuss.
- Make plans to include your daughter in your busy life in ways that will (hopefully) be positive for both of you.

Notes

celebrate the moment

normalize respect

Our family attended a wedding reception some years ago at which one of the guests walked over to where we were talking with his wife. He spoke to her in a derogatory way and then reached for her breast. He squeezed it right in front of us before walking off, announcing that he was going to get a piece of wedding cake. His wife let out a twittering laugh.

"Boys will be boys," she said with a shrug.

I was in shock. My expression must have suggested that I was in pain, because later, when my husband and I talked about it, he said it had looked like I was going to cry.

"I *did* feel like I was about to cry," I replied. "No woman should ever be treated that way. Especially by her husband and in public!"

What followed was a long family conversation about respect and honor. My husband and I got an education on how our kids' peers talked to and treated each other at school. Our kids talked openly about modern music lyrics and popular expressions. My heart ached.

In that moment, I ignored my own advice about using Listening Language. I broke into full-on lecture mode, because I felt desperate for my young-adult children to recognize normal and acceptable behavior, regardless of what they'd seen or heard elsewhere. I told them that I expected them to go against the flow and always be respectful of others as well as their own bodies—and to accept nothing less from anyone else.

Looking back on that conversation, I am convinced that the moms and dads of this generation have an even greater responsibility to instill a sense of honor and respect in their sons and daughters. It's not a quality that is typically modeled in their circles or in our culture at large.

Many moms have told me about the struggles they experience once their daughter gets her own phone. One mom said her daughter became obsessed with selfies, filters, video sharing, and perfecting her poses. Her self-image became so fragile that her parents made the difficult decision to radically limit her screen time.

"If we'd known what we'd be exposing her to," the mom told me, "we would have waited a few more years before getting her a phone, even though she would have begged for one continually. We would have used those preteen years to get her involved in activities that would boost her confidence and help her establish her identity, so she'd see herself the way God views her. All that influence mixed with those early puberty hormone swings was not good for her. The main thing we're focusing on now is helping her respect herself."

When a young woman respects herself, she behaves and makes decisions from a place of strength and dignity rather than shrugging off or even emulating the unacceptable behavior of others.

What does it take to normalize respect among our kids? It takes parents who start the conversation with their children at a young age and keep it going as they grow and are exposed to more outside influences. Don't despair if you haven't already started that discussion. Begin with your daughter now, however old she is, and help her understand her true value. Teach her how she should be treated.

> "Strength and dignity are her clothing, and she smiles at the future."
> Proverbs 31:25, NASB

I've always liked the imagery of *The Living Bible* blessing found in Psalm 144:12, which refers to "daughters of graceful beauty like the pillars of a palace wall." (Other translations liken them to "stately columns.") When we raise our daughters to be like strong pillars or stately columns, they become women who hold up "palaces." They stand firm with strength and beauty. They are the structural elements that help keep families, businesses, and communities in place. Their distinct beauty is the first thing a visitor notices. Without their powerful support, the structures would crumble.

So don't mess with my beautiful pillar of a daughter. Strength and dignity are her clothing. She has reason to smile at the future.

Your Conversation Plan

How can you protect your daughter's innocence while at the same time prepare her for the adult world? Respect is essential, and so is open communication. Keep doing all the things you're doing now to filter out harmful influences. Protect her imagination.

At the same time, keep the conversation door wide open so she can come to you whenever she's presented with unknown words, images, and information. Don't worry about saying things "just so"—use language that feels comfortable to both of you.

I remember when our son came home after playing with some neighborhood kids and tried out a new word he had just heard. Trust me, that word should not be included in any nine-year-old's vocabulary. I asked if he knew what it meant. He said no, but it had made the other boys laugh. So he repeated it and they laughed again.

Instead of discussing the word's crude meaning, I told him that it described a disrespectful way to treat another person. I left out any anatomical facts or explanations because I wanted to protect his imagination. I told him that our family didn't use that term and that the other boys laughed because they knew it was a disrespectful thing to say.

My son seemed satisfied with my explanation, and the rest of our conversation turned to how important it is to show respect to others.

When I thought about it later, I was glad I didn't automatically use terms like *dirty* or *nasty*. There's nothing dirty or nasty about God's creation. Reproduction in all its forms is miraculous because it comes from God.

When God made the stars, whales, and daffodils, He said they were "good." When God made humans—man and woman, male and female—He said they were "very good." Our bodies are part of the "very good" of God's creation. We were created above the other living things. Our bodies are meant to be shared in gloriously delightful ways within the sacred gift of marriage.

One of the ways you can protect your daughter's innocence, as well as her imagination, is by not referring to any part of the body as "nasty." Elevate your conversations by expressing respect for every human. Emphasize all that is honorable and make sure your daughter only hears respect when you refer to anything sexual.

Body Image

I realize that this might be an uncomfortable topic for some. But I hope you'll keep reading, because if you can be comfortable talking about your body in a respectful way, it will help set the tone for a better future for your daughter and her self-image.

For some women, just thinking about respectful, appropriate touching can trigger painful memories. If you are one of those women, I understand. When those painful memories come rushing back, they can bring with them a mental and emotional paralysis stemming from childhood or young-adult experiences. The mere thought of speaking about these topics with your daughter can feel overwhelming.

So please be gentle with yourself. Take this process step by step. I want you to be able to move forward and experience the healing that God offers for your life.

If you've never addressed past issues of abuse, shame, self-hatred, or injustice, I urge you to seek help. Tell your story to a trusted and professional counselor. Set your heart toward being healed and whole.

I went to a skilled Christian counselor when our children were almost teens. I'd gone to a medical doctor first, and he diagnosed my symptoms as premenopausal. I went on a search for ways to balance my hormones, then I made an appointment with a qualified counselor and talked about the memories that wouldn't go away.

He responded with truth that both hurt and helped. I remember coming home after one of these sessions feeling exhausted. I longed for a verse to cling to that I could read over and over. This passage in Philippians became an anchor as the emotional waves crashed all around me: "Brothers and sisters, I do not regard myself as having taken hold of it yet; but one thing I do: forgetting what lies behind and reaching forward to what lies ahead" (Philippians 3:13, NASB).

After completing several sessions with the counselor, my physical and emotional anxieties began to lift. I realized that the pieces of my past I had once labeled as broken and unusable were actually something beautiful because they came out of the redeemable heap of humanity where we all reside. Those broken shards, with their irregular edges, were reshaped and reformed as I exposed them to the light of God's truth.

By taking those broken pieces out of hiding and putting them all on the table—like puzzle pieces—the counselor helped me put my life back together. All the fractured pieces had a place. My life still told a story, but it was no longer a story of shame.

We are all familiar with darkness. We are good at hiding, you and me. Retreating from the light is a tale as old as Adam and Eve. Remember how they hid from God in the Garden of Eden? Their first instinct was to withdraw, to cover up, to avoid their own shame by not being seen or known.

That didn't stop God from coming to the Garden, seeking them out, and calling, "Where are you?"

I believe God still walks in the cool of the evening through the garden of our heart. He still calls out that same question to us: "Where are you?"

Adam replied that they had hidden because they were ashamed. The relationship between God and Adam and Eve could not move forward until they came out of hiding, revealed what had happened, and received what God had for them in the next season of life.

I've seen this pattern repeated many times over the years in my relationship with God. I mess up, I get messed up, I feel strangled by shame, and I go into hiding. I hide from people and from God.

The moment I come out of hiding—when I confess, open

up, tell the truth, and draw near to God—that's when I move forward on a redemptive path that leads out of the darkness and into the light. That path always leads me to freedom. Always.

The reconstructed puzzle pieces of our broken lives always tell a story. It's a one-of-a-kind story of how everything is redeemable with God. Something beautiful can be made from the broken shards.

I dearly want you to walk in freedom as you come alongside your daughter and lead her into this next season of her life. I want you to feel a sense of dignity and restored respect for your own body as well as hers as you move forward. Establishing a foundation of respect will influence every conversation with your daughter, which is why I believe that foundation needs to be in place before discussing the details of how her body is changing.

Essentials for Self-Respect

Right now, no matter her age, is the best time to instill a sense of value and self-respect in your daughter. I know some of you moms are more detail-oriented than I am, and you might already have a list of ten essential topics you want to cover with your daughter before she's ten. But if you have no such list, the two respect-inducing topics I've listed below are a decent starting point.

Just make sure you don't overwhelm your daughter in an attempt to be thorough. Pay attention to how she responds. Only answer the questions she asks, not the ones she hasn't yet considered. Try to move at her pace, even if you're well-supplied with information and suggestions.

1. Our Amazing Bodies
   - Even as toddlers, kids can understand from books and educational shows just how intricately God made us. Is your daughter curious about how her lungs work? Fascinated by hearing her heartbeat through a stethoscope? Nurture her curiosity.
   - Nurture the wonder of her body. Tell her how strong her arms are, what pretty fingers she has, and how much you love her smile. Compliment her and help her come to love features that someone else has commented on in a negative way.
   - Use anatomically correct terms for body parts. This conveys respect, while slang terms are demeaning.
   - Express a sense of acceptance and appreciation for your own body. Being kind to yourself in front of her teaches a powerful lesson without delivering a single lecture on self-esteem. Show rather than just tell your daughter how a woman should feel about herself.

2. Her Privacy
   - Experts say a good general guideline for your children is that no one should touch or see the parts of their body that would be covered by underwear or a bathing suit. (There are exceptions for doctors and others, of course, but this is a good place to start.)

- Assure your daughter that she has every right to defend and protect herself if her privacy feels threatened or if someone demonstrates disrespect for her body. (My husband taught our daughter several self-defense moves when she was young. Thankfully she never had to use them, but she was prepared to protect the privacy of her own body.)
- Allow your daughter the privacy of a closed door, a chance to be alone, space to cry, or the opportunity to burn off steam before asking her to tell you what she's upset about.

You can cover most of these key topics at any age. Yet the sooner you begin, the easier it will be when the time comes to broach deeper subjects. Some conversations are more free-flowing when you're side by side in a car, but others are better served by being face to face. That way you can both catch the nuances in your expressions. Talking about these essential topics early on will help your daughter see that she can always talk to you about the important things in life, and that those conversations will be natural and respectful.

Respect Demonstrated in a Group

I described in an earlier chapter how some women put together a special event for all the fifth-grade girls at their church. Their younger sisters could barely wait until it was their turn to attend the Girls Are Amazing party.

The event included a sleepover with silly games, music,

sleeping bags, and pj's along with lots of fun, food, and laughter. Several women whom the girls looked up to gave engaging talks on skin care, modesty, friendships, hygiene, and—most importantly—what God has to say about their value. The next morning they had a hands-on cooking class with a female chef who also discussed healthy eating habits. The girls went home with a gift bag filled with simple, healthy recipes; shampoo samples; bookmarks with Bible verses; and a gift card to their local Christian bookstore.

The event was designed to work in tandem with what the girls' mothers were doing to prepare them for puberty. It was *not* designed to take the place of the important conversations a mom should have with her daughter, but rather as a positive "bonus" conversation that supported what the parents were already doing to make their daughter's journey into womanhood an exciting and honoring experience.

Once again, it's all about starting with a foundation of respect. The women who put together the event honored the families, the daughters, and the core idea that the process is different for each girl. Their mission was to create a welcoming community environment for these young girls and to affirm that becoming a woman is an amazing adventure.

Wouldn't you have loved an event like that when you were in fifth grade? I would have probably considered it among the absolute best memories of my early adolescence.

I especially appreciate that the women who organized these gatherings saw the importance of talking to the girls about their value in Christ. I've been writing books for teen girls for decades and have received thousands of letters from readers. One consistent theme in those letters is how the readers view God and their questions about how He views them.

They've shared many misconceptions with me. Many of them became stuck at an early age in thinking that God would be mad at them if they didn't do everything in life the right way. Others have written to me about their lofty aspirations. They even used the words "I just want to make God and my parents proud of me."

To all those young women I want to say, "Shame *off* you. Grace *on* you."

Did you catch that? Shame off, grace on.

I've included those words in books I've written and in talks I've given, and I have heard the reactions of hundreds of girls. Many of their comments kept coming to mind as I wrote a nonfiction book for teen girls titled *Spoken For*. I coauthored the book with Alyssa Bethke because we both wanted to tell girls how valuable they are to God. He's not waiting with a lightning bolt to strike you when you sin. Nor is He waiting for you to do something heroic that will make Him proud of you.

God doesn't respond to our choices with clenched fists, suggesting that He wants to "get back at you." Instead, He responds with open arms and welcoming, nail-pierced hands because He wants to "get you back." His love is unfailing. It's multifaceted and beautifully tender.

If you are intentional about normalizing respect by teaching it and modeling it for your daughter, you'll be amazed to see how self-confident she becomes as she heads into puberty.

Dear Robin . . .

*Both of my parents are reserved, but they did two things
that made me feel like they cared about me and respected
my feelings during my early adolescent years.*

*First, they read through the entire Christy Miller High
School Years series with me at night. They took turns
reading a chapter at bedtime. Sometimes we had to read
two chapters because of the cliff-hangers! They asked me
nonthreatening questions like "Do you know any guys like
Todd?" or "What would you do if you were Christy, and
Alissa left you at the party?" or "Do you have a friend who
acts like Katie?"*

*We had the best conversations. I've always been grateful
for that time with my parents and the way the fictional role
models in the stories went through all the same things I went
through with friends, first love, school, and my family. It
was as if Christy's pretend stories gave me an open door to
talk to my parents about my own real-life story.*

*The second thing my mom did well was to have "the
talk" with me in a natural, almost scientific way. That's
what felt most comfortable and respectful to her. When I
started my period, I already had everything I needed, and
I knew what was happening. I told my mom right away.
She gave me a big hug and asked if it was okay with me if
she told my dad. I said she could because it felt natural for
him to be included in the moment.*

*That night my dad came home with a big bouquet of
carnations for me. It was kind of like his way of reenacting*

the scene in Summer Promise *when Todd gave Christy
the carnations, only mine were pink. When he gave me the
bouquet, he said, "Now that you're a woman, I wanted to
be the first man to give you flowers and tell you how much
I love you."*

*It's one of my favorite childhood/young adulthood
memories. My parents didn't need to say much. I knew
I was loved, protected, and respected.*

Start Now

What are some ways you might put the ideas from this chapter
into action? What portions of the chapter stood out to you?
Here are some possible points of action:

- Ask your daughter what words of loving affirmation
from her heavenly Father she sees in each of the verses.
Be sure to listen to her first and then add your thoughts
on how the verse affects the way you view yourself in
light of how God sees you.
- If you're good at organizing, get together with some
other moms to plan your own version of a Girls Are
Amazing event, whether large or small.
- Make a plan with your husband, mom, sisters, or friends
ahead of time regarding how they might participate in
the rite-of-passage moment with your daughter. They
can do this by having a card or letter ready for you to
hand to your girl or a small gift such as the bouquet
from her dad described above. That way you've invited
the other important adults in your daughter's life to be
part of an affirming circle.

- If you're married and haven't done so yet, have a private conversation with your husband. Tell him about your own experience with puberty, and come up with some ways you can affirm your daughter together in this season of change. Assure him that a young girl needs hugs and compliments from her dad so that she does not seek them from another male.

Notes

before your tween daughter becomes a woman

make peace with your past

It's important for me to add this chapter about your past because it all starts with you.

You know that, right?

You might have had an easy, or at least easy-*ish*, journey through adolescence. Your relationship with your mom may have been close then and might be even closer now. You were nurtured well and, so far, this book has provided you with some fun ideas for how you can keep the love and affection going into the next generation with your daughter.

If that's your story, then what a gift you were given.

For other women, the past is more complicated. Their relationship with their mom wasn't ideal, and the hurts have stayed with them well into this next season of life. If that's you, don't skip this chapter. It will help you make peace with your past. I want you to be able to enter into these important conversations with your daughter with an uncluttered heart.

What do I mean by an uncluttered heart?

You know how renovation experts on TV shows can walk into a house and right away know which walls can or should be removed to open up the floor plan? They knock out old walls and install new, more efficient beams. They pull up stained carpets and bring the original wood floors back to life. By the end of the show, the house is transformed into a spacious, breathing, light-filled, inviting home.

Think of your heart in the same way. Do you have walls that need to come down? What's under that old carpet you've tread upon for years? Which windows need to be replaced?

The work begins on demo day. That's when it's time to put on your goggles and pick up your sledgehammer—when you get down to the framework by recalling what it was like when your own body changed. Let's go there now.

Your Story

Start by answering these questions:

1. How old were you when you started your period?
2. How much did you understand about what was happening?
3. What did you not understand about what your body was doing?

4. Did you have any questions that you felt unable to ask?
5. What concerns did you have about the changes in your body?

If you and I were having this conversation over a nice cuppa breakfast tea, I can assure you that I'd be interested in hearing your answers. I've been listening to coming-of-age stories for many years—and at this point, I think I've heard it all. There's almost nothing you could say that would shock me.

But since you and I are not having this conversation face to face, is there someone you do feel comfortable talking with? Is there another mom, mentor, sister, or good friend who excels at listening and sharing? Start by asking each other the five questions above. You'll find that it can be surprisingly helpful to share your answers about these important life moments with a kindred spirit.

Taking time to contemplate your childhood experiences can do several things for you. First, it will increase your empathy for your daughter because—and let's be honest—when was the last time you tried to remember how you felt when you were her age?

Second, an important part of this exercise is to help you not get stuck in the past, but rather to focus on what is ahead for your daughter. You want to open the door to the possibility of a better future relationship with her.

Making peace with your past is a process. Healing is a process. Forgiveness is a process. When it comes to your past, give yourself space and grace. Remain open throughout the journey and keep taking those baby steps. Don't close off your heart.

A wise friend once told me that I should take time to take an inventory of my journey into womanhood. She suggested this when my daughter was still a toddler, because my friend said I needed to make sure I didn't turn into a walking-wounded mom who transferred my own childhood hurts onto my daughter without realizing it.

At the time I struggled with her advice, but she was right. It was important. Getting my heart uncluttered made a significant difference in both my life and my daughter's life. I had to do the hard work of looking over my shoulder, releasing past hurts, and setting my heart and mind on what was ahead. That vital process stripped away the anger and sense of humiliation I'd carried for years.

As a result, I'm able to tell the story of my entrance into puberty in an open and honest way without shrinking back in shame or getting tangled up in processing all those early-adolescence emotions alongside the facts.

I'd like to share my journey with you now in hopes that it will help you think through your own experience. The sooner you can separate the truths from the lies and begin to heal from past hurts, the sooner you'll be free to start telling yourself your story in a liberating way. You'll be in a much healthier place mentally, spiritually, and emotionally as you enter into this next season of your daughter's life. Think of your healing as a gift she'll never know you gave her.

I Was Ten

My period started the second week of fifth grade during recess. I went to the bathroom and couldn't figure out where the blood was coming from. I folded up a lot of toilet paper and hoped it would go away.

By the second day, the cramping frightened me. I thought something was seriously wrong—like maybe I was dying! I finally went to my mom at the end of that day and told her I was bleeding.

"Get a Band-Aid," she said in her matter-of-fact way.

"I don't think we have any that are big enough."

"Why not?"

"Because . . ." I burst into tears and couldn't finish.

"What are you crying about?"

"It's coming from . . ." I pointed, still crying.

The look on my mom's face was complicated. I read it as partly surprise but mostly disgust. All she said was, "Don't you know what that is?"

I shook my head. I had no idea what was happening. No clue at all. None of my friends had matured as quickly as I had. No one I knew talked openly about such things.

"It's the curse," she mumbled. "Go to your room."

I was confused. *The curse?* Had I done something wrong? The shame I felt was suffocating.

My flustered mother came in a few minutes later with a box of pads and a booklet. "Take this to the bathroom," she said. "Read it and take a shower before you use these."

I complied. An hour later I tried to act natural at the dinner table with my parents, my brother, and my sister. My mother didn't say anything. I would have been mortified if she had. We acted as if everything were normal.

Except it wasn't normal. Nothing felt natural. My body was doing strange things. I was sitting on a thick pad that felt odd and uncomfortable. My mind was still processing clinical drawings of Fallopian tubes and a uterus from a booklet that was held together by a single staple. I was so naïve. I never knew I was carrying around eggs. What in the world was sperm, and how did it get into a woman's uterus? I had so many questions. I felt overwhelmed and alone.

This was before the internet, so I couldn't privately Google my questions. Siri wasn't there to help me. I didn't know anyone I could ask, so I shut down inside.

My entrance to womanhood began with fear, shame, and isolation. What I learned that day was that growing up was something I had to figure out on my own. The pattern was set: I rarely went to my mom to ask her anything ever again.

During my high school years, I turned to friends, magazines, and books for information and advice. The unspoken message that came through clearly when I was ten and terrified was that if I ever again went to my mother with a problem or a question, she would scowl at my immaturity and squelch discussion of any sort.

I knew I wanted my relationship with my children to be the opposite of what I'd experienced. I wanted my children to feel that they could always come to me about anything.

But before that could happen, I had some internal work to do.

An Uncluttered Heart

For several decades I placed all the responsibility on my mother for our distant, seemingly uncaring relationship. If any one person in this whole world should show their love and care by always being there for you, it should be your mother, right?

That was not the case for me. Something had to change before I could become the caring mom I wanted to be for my daughter. The first step was to make sure I didn't harbor any unforgiveness toward my own mother.

I don't know much about what my mom experienced during her childhood. She never talked about it. It wasn't possible for me to understand her pain, her struggles, or why her approach to many things came from a deep well of disapproval. She had a critical spirit, and in my twenties I was certain that I was nothing like her.

In my early thirties, however, during my second pregnancy, I heard myself lashing out at my mom with a bitter, cruel response when she pushed my buttons. It shocked me to realize that I sounded just like her.

Now I was the one who had dug deep wells of resentment and filled them to the brim with the poison that was seeping out to those around me. I realized that I was angry at my mom all the time. I didn't want any sort of relationship with her.

My husband said I turned into a different person when I was around her. I reverted to passive-aggressive tactics, like muttering negative comments under my breath or over-apologizing and acting as if it were a given fact that I couldn't do anything right. I withdrew and coddled my hurts.

Something had to change.

I remember the afternoon when I poured out my heart to God. I asked Him to forgive me and to release me from my bitterness toward my mom. I remember saying aloud . . .

"No more!"

It was as if I'd drawn a line and told all the hurt from the past that it was no longer allowed to cross that boundary—no longer permitted to influence my present or my future. The dark-winged vulture of self-pity had to fly away. Shame no longer had access to my heart. I asked God to remove all the resentment and hurt—to fling it back into the pit it had come from. No more oppression, only freedom. I wanted to become the mom my children needed me to be.

As I prayed, I asked God to fill me with truth—truth about His unfailing love for me and His extravagant grace. So much grace! I asked God to teach me how to extend that same abundant grace to myself, to my little family, and especially to my mom.

The healing process began immediately.

Notice that I said "process." Lots of ups and downs occurred as the years went on. But almost immediately I felt a sense of release. I stopped expecting or even hoping to receive nurturing from my mom. I accepted her as she was and knew that the most important choices in our relationship now belonged to me. I could withhold kindness, affection, and loving care from her, or I could recognize what she was either not willing or not able to give to me.

Grace and unconditional love became my new superpowers

in this renovated relationship with my mother. I wrote in my journal that I wanted to be "remembered for what I do, not what was done to me."

The more I chose to let go of the irritations and not return the jabs, the more empowered I became. Soon I was the one who directed our conversations and responded to my mom out of love. I stopped keeping a list of wrongs. I stopped envying relationships my friends had with their moms. Most importantly, I stopped expecting different results.

Consider that popular definition of *insanity*—"doing the same thing over and over again but expecting a different result." Well, I stopped doing that. I got my sanity back, and I suddenly found a whole lot of open space in my heart where God filled me with His love and His lavish gift of grace.

> "Be gentle and ready to forgive; never hold grudges. Remember, the Lord forgave you, so you must forgive others."
> Colossians 3:13, TLB

When He fills you up, there is more than enough love and grace for you to give to others. I've never run out of love for my mom, because my love for her was a result of God's unconditional love for me. Best of all, I was able to approach my married and parenting years with plenty of love and grace for my husband and children. I could be intentional about the family patterns that needed to change in my generation and focus on establishing a new foundation.

Start the Process

When you glance over your shoulder to look at your past, does it all seem like too much to deal with? Does "uncluttering" sound too idealistic? Maybe you think that a major bulldozing would be a more realistic approach.

Okay, fine. Go get a bulldozer. Whatever it takes, just move forward! Don't get stuck. Don't put off your own healing. Take time to step away from the rush of daily life and dig deep into the lasting truth of God's Word. Schedule an appointment with a qualified counselor. Have a heart-to-heart conversation with a mentor or close friend, someone who will listen and pray for you. Whatever it takes, do it.

You know how to find resources. You know what you need. Take the necessary steps to become healed, whole, and unhindered by your past. You want to be available to family, friends, and loved ones. You need to be free to focus on the *now*—not bogged down by past hurts. Self-pity is the worst. It can cripple you.

A big aha moment for me came when I was watching *Sleepless in Seattle*. The actress Rita Wilson was performing a scene in which she was crying about the classic movie *An Affair to Remember*, specifically the scene in which Cary Grant comes to visit Deborah Kerr at the end of the film. Grant's character doesn't understand why Kerr's character didn't meet him at the Empire State Building as they had agreed. And why didn't she stand up and embrace him? Instead, she remained on a couch with a blanket over her legs. He has no idea she'd been disabled in an auto accident.

I cried along with Rita because I realized that all these years I'd been emotionally standing there, not understanding, waiting for my mother to get up and come to me. I had no idea that she simply couldn't.

Yet I could go to her. I could choose to remain in the room, in the relationship. I could take her just as she was and choose to love her in her emotionally disabled state.

"I love you" were words my mom didn't use much while I was growing up. They are powerful words, and I decided to say them to her once my heart was uncluttered and I felt filled up with God's love and grace. I looked her in the eyes and said, "I love you."

She turned away and didn't respond.

I thought about her reaction for a while and decided it was okay. Even if she never said those words back to me, I found that I was free to say them to her, from my heart, whenever I felt compelled to do so. And I did.

I'll never forget a phone call with my mom when I was in my early fifties. I ended it with the same, "I love you, Mom," that I'd been saying to her out of sincerity for almost a decade. But that day, she returned those words.

"I love you, too."

It makes my heart happy to tell you that I've now heard my mom tell me many times that she loves me. Not from the beginning, but at the end of her days. The truth and power of sincere love covered a multitude of past hurts and led us to the process we both went through as we experienced God's healing. Each time she said those words, I received them.

The Oxygen-Mask Example

Yes, you've probably heard this example before. But it absolutely applies here, so I'm going to remind you of it again. When you deal with your issues and needs *first*, you can then give your children what they need. You might even be able to give your mom something she has always needed. In that way, addressing your self-care first is a lot like the safety instructions repeated by every flight attendant before the plane takes off: "In case of an emergency, place your oxygen mask over your nose and mouth *first* before assisting your child."

One could say that our culture and our families are all in a state of emergency today. So many influences stand ready to hijack our relationships with our daughters—or worse, take us both down in flames. The rules of airline preparedness apply: Take care of yourself first, *then* help your daughter with what she needs.

The greatest truth in all this is that God can do anything. He can set you free in the unseen realm, where chains of shame, guilt, anger, unforgiveness, and resentment may have plagued the women in your family for generations.

Please be the one who breaks the cycle and says, "No more." Reach for your oxygen mask first.

A new path begins with you, for you, and through you. This new pattern will define not only your daughter's passage into womanhood but also—don't overlook this—your freedom from the past that can affect all the women in your family lineage. Women yet to be born might be affected by the choices you make today. Pretty astounding, isn't it?

If you're not sure how to begin this internal spring cleaning, try starting with this prayer from Psalm 51:10: "Create in me a clean heart, O God; and renew a right spirit within me" (KJV). ·

Dear Robin . . .
I heard you talk about your experience with your mother when you were growing up, and it helped me feel like I wasn't the only one who took a while to move into a decent relationship with her mom.
    My mom always made a big deal about everything. She loved putting on celebrations. But I'm a private person and never liked her grand parties. I learned when I was young that if I told her anything personal, she would tell everyone. It's how her big family did things. I'm more like my dad, quiet and shy. He loves my mom and her vivacious personality, so I always saw them as an opposites-attract sort of couple. But growing up, I never felt secure around my mom.
    I was eleven when I started my period. I knew plenty already because everything was discussed openly in our house. What terrified me was the thought of what my mom might say or do when I told her. So I didn't. I was so frightened that I remained silent for months and months and found ways to take care of everything I needed without her knowing.
    I felt so guilty. When I was twelve, I wrote her a letter saying that I kept it a secret because I couldn't deal with the attention that I knew she would want to place on me.

I remember thinking I was so mature because in my letter I told her I had trust issues.

She was hurt, and for the next decade we pretty much kept our distance from each other. I know it was painful for both of us, but I didn't know how to change the patterns that had been set.

When I was twenty-one, I started seeing a female Christian counselor. Those sessions were a turning point in my life. I wrote my mom another letter at the end of my last counseling session. This time I thanked her for all the ways she had loved me and had been a caring mom, and I invited her to meet me for lunch. I couldn't believe how much we cleared up during those two hours. For the first time I felt like she accepted me just the way I was, as an introvert. I think I began to understand and accept her, too.

When I turned twenty-five, she wanted to throw me a big party, and believe it or not, I told her I would like that. It was the best party. It really was. She loved it, and so did I. I felt like I had entered a new season with her, and all the anxiety from my timid preteen years was no longer an issue.

I'm grateful for our renovated relationship. I don't know what my life would be like if I didn't have my mom in it the way she is now. I've learned that it's never too late to try to connect with your mom.

Start Now

What are some ways you might put the ideas from this chapter into action? What portions of the chapter stood out to you? Here are some possible points of action:

- Take time to evaluate where you are in your relationship with your mother.
- Consider how you can settle the unresolved issues from your childhood.
- Talk to someone who understands and can help you make peace with your past.
- Spend time praying, releasing, and forgiving those who treated you unfairly.
- Don't return to unhealthy "thought ruts" you've tromped through over the years.
- Create new thought patterns and do your part to restore broken relationships.
- Strap on your own oxygen mask first before helping your daughter.

Notes

before your tween daughter becomes a woman

focus on the future

Your heavenly Father has been with you from the beginning of your existence—and the beginning of your daughter's existence. He is already at work in this season of your life and your daughter's life. He is able to do more than you could ever imagine. More than you could ever dream.

This is the truth that fills all of us moms with hope.

By taking the time to read this book and think about what's best for your daughter, you are already focusing on the future. You are pouring all kinds of goodness, grace, truth, and love into the next generation.

Once again I applaud you. Well done.

Now what about that small matter of sharing the details of

your past and your experiences with your girl? What does she need to know about your childhood? What will help, and what might hurt?

This is the time for you to think about what you want to share and how to do it in a way that will enrich your daughter's life.

Think of all the good times in your childhood. Remember the sweet memories and let those good things serve as the opening lines of your conversation. Pour out all the happy stories and the sweet memories. Don't hold back. Share the simple joys that shaped you during your early years. Recall the kind things that were done to you and for you. Give out of the abundance that was given to you.

When your thoughts turn to childhood hurts, and if you know that one day you'll want to share deeper, more complex memories with your daughter, I hope you'll spend some time going through this chapter. Think about the big picture and what really matters.

The following three questions are the ones I've been asked most often. I hope my replies will give you some encouraging insights. I know you want to make wise choices with your words. You want to turn the focus toward what is to come and not get stuck on what came before.

1. HOW MUCH SHOULD I TELL MY DAUGHTER ABOUT MY OWN EXPERIENCES AS A YOUNG GIRL?

Please start slowly. Your daughter doesn't need to know everything about your life when she's seven. She really doesn't. And she especially doesn't need to feel as if everything that happens in her life is measured against the yardstick of your experiences. Who among us likes to hear statements that begin with "When I was your age . . ."?

If your growing-up years include significant events you've had to process in-depth, then measure out those details little by little. Only share what's necessary. Guard her innocence.

A friend of mine answered her seven-year-old daughter's question about who someone was in an old family photo by saying, "That's your grandpa's brother."

She was prepared to add ". . . and he was mean to my sister and me when we were little. He did things to us that he shouldn't have. It was really sad."

However, she caught herself and realized that nothing more needed to be said. She could always give her daughter more details when she was older if it would genuinely benefit her to hear the whole story. But this wasn't the time to tell a little girl about childhood abuse and a court trial that divided the family and sent her uncle to prison for four years.

What mattered at the moment was that, as a mom, she knew how to be alert and protect her daughter—and how to train her daughter to protect herself. The reasons why she was so in tune with those instincts didn't need to be the starting point of a growing and ongoing conversation.

Think of the way you share the truth with your daughter in terms of how much salt is needed to make a delicious batch of cookies. You only need a quarter teaspoon, not two cups. Just a sprinkle. Salt may be part of the recipe, but it's not the key ingredient. Likewise, your past experiences are part of your relationship with your daughter, but they aren't the main ingredient.

During her preadolescent years, you're crafting a recipe for how your communication will grow and continue in the years to come. If you've produced a bad batch, so to speak, due to too much salt and not enough sugar, that's okay. You can always start over. Pay closer attention to your measurements this time. In the same way, keep working at it with your daughter until your recipe for communication has just the right combination of ingredients.

What is the key ingredient? I believe it should be grace. Big scoops of grace for you and heaping cups full of grace for your daughter.

You know how some recipes say, "Mix in a separate bowl" or "Divide the yolks from the egg whites"? That same step-by-step process of separating might be part of your personal family recipe. Grace allows you to separate your relationship with your mom from your daughter's relationship with both of you. It allows you to process and heal from past hurts in your own bowl while preparing a different part of your daughter's life recipe in another bowl.

Remember that you're putting your own oxygen mask on first. You're uncluttering your own heart and not forcing your daughter to go through that process with you. Much like stained glass, all the broken pieces of your life can be arranged together so that, when the light shines through, it tells a beautiful story.

You probably have a lot going on in your own season of life. All of it will eventually be sifted and mixed into your daughter's life. For now, though, please don't dump everything on her at once.

Like many families, we have a few people in our clan who have demonstrated by their life choices that they are not the safest people for our kids to be around. In those cases, we provided uncomplicated explanations for our children regarding why we stepped away or limited our time with them. We wanted our children to learn how to be discerning and, at the same time, confident that we wouldn't place them in a situation where it was up to them to protect themselves.

As my daughter grew older, she tuned in to some of the ways my mom disapproved of things I said or did. That's when she felt her own tug-of-war with her grandma and made self-protecting adjustments along the way. As Rachel shared with me her feelings about her grandma, I shared more of my own feelings and experiences.

By that time I'd healed a lot and wasn't trying to get my daughter on my side nor use her as a therapist. It really is possible to speak the truth in love when you've first done the important work of uncluttering your heart.

As you work on your communication recipe with your daughter, especially regarding your past experiences, please remember that most fluctuating preteens haven't yet developed a balanced sense of understanding and discernment. That maturity will come, but be patient.

If I had unloaded all my experiences, opinions, and feelings on Rachel when she was still a little girl, she would have not only felt overwhelmed but would also have missed out on experiencing her own important moments with her grandma, other relatives, and family friends. It was my responsibility to separate out my feelings and let her develop her own opinions and relationships.

2. HOW DO I KNOW WHAT TO SAY TO MY DAUGHTER?

The quick answer here is to pray for wisdom, as James 1:5 encourages us to do:

> Now if any of you lacks wisdom, he should ask God,
> who gives to all generously and without criticizing, and
> it will be given to him.
>
> JAMES 1:5, HCSB

Prayer is always the best first step for a parent in any situation, no matter how old your children are. Whenever possible, give yourself enough space to think through and pray about what you want and need to say, as well as how and when you should initiate the topic.

A friend of mine had a complicated journey through her teen years. She planned to share openly with her daughter how she had become pregnant at fifteen and about the fear-driven choice she had made in isolation to end the pregnancy. Over the years she has made peace with her past and knows that God has redeemed her and brought good out of that painful time in her life.

Unfortunately, instead of having the freedom to share her story with her daughter at the time and in the way she wanted, a relative chose to enlighten the girl when she was nine years old. She came to her mother in tears, asking, "Why did you kill our baby?" My friend stopped everything and sat down with her. This is how she described that difficult conversation:

"I started by telling her that my childhood was quite different from hers. I didn't have anyone I could talk to, and I didn't understand how my body worked or how overwhelming my emotions could be. I told her I kept making poor choices that led to more bad choices. I was very sorry for those decisions, I said, but I knew that God forgave me when I asked Him to.

"It was a really difficult conversation, and all the way through I kept asking God to give me wisdom. The thought that kept coming to me was that I needed to use discretion. I knew I could give her more details later if I needed to. But in that intense moment, I only needed to say enough to let my daughter know that she could always come to me to talk about difficult things and be assured that I would tell her the truth."

Since that first painful conversation, my friend and her daughter have had half a dozen more open discussions about sexual intimacy, peer pressure, fear-based choices, and the sanctity of life. Even though the conversation started in an unwelcome way, my friend is grateful for the closeness it created. Her daughter is now fifteen and experiencing a far different adolescence than my friend did because of the big-picture discussions that helped her understand how to make good choices.

3. THINGS ARE DIFFERENT NOW THAN WHEN I WAS MY DAUGHTER'S AGE. SHE KNOWS SO MUCH MORE THAN I DID. WHY SHOULDN'T I GET EVERYTHING OUT INTO THE OPEN?

It's true—and kind of sad—that modern culture and communication have changed so dramatically since you were ten years old. But one thing hasn't changed: the elegance of discretion.

Have you ever heard the phrase "a word fitly spoken"? It comes from Proverbs 25:11. I like how *The Message* paraphrase expresses that passage: "The right word at the right time is like a custom-made piece of jewelry."

Isn't that a good image? Choosing the best thing to say at the right time is as considerate as giving a beautiful gift that was made especially for that person.

I learned how beautiful discretion can be when I spent time with a woman named Ethel. She was older than me, and in due time, she became my writing mentor. She was an established author when we first met, and I was still trying to get my first article published. I hadn't even started writing a book, yet I blithely approached her with a long list of questions about what it was like to be an author and what I needed to do to get published.

She answered very few of my questions with specific details. Instead, Ethel graciously invited me to join a writer's critique group she hosted at her home. For six years we met once a month, and little by little she taught me the essentials of the writing craft. As our friendship grew, I realized how bold I'd been when I'd first approached her as a starry-eyed novice. Yet she patiently measured out the realities of writing for publication step by step, with discretion.

Our friendship continued for several decades, and Ethel became a sheltering tree for me. The rains still came, but because of her closeness, I wasn't doused all at once. We confided in each other, and she shared about the losses, injustices, and disappointments she had experienced in the publishing world. With every setback or failure that I experienced, I knew I could share them all with her because she understood.

I look back now and see that if Ethel had given me all her insights, experiences, and gut-level truths at one time, I would have been overwhelmed. I might have become so discouraged that I would have given up before finishing my first novel.

But I wasn't overwhelmed or jaded by the process because Ethel exercised the beautiful gift of discretion. I didn't need to know everything at once. I didn't need to carry with me the disappointments and rejections she had experienced on her journey. I could go at my own pace, knowing that she walked beside me and would answer each question with just the right combination of information and discretion.

Ethel was my mentor—the person who gave me the tools and information I needed so I could make the best choices for my future. As you mentor your own daughter, always consider how you might guard her heart. You are her sheltering tree. Give her the tools she needs to make good choices for herself.

Discretion isn't a common topic, is it? It's more likely you've heard the popular opinion that we have the right to speak openly about everything that happens to us, and if people don't want us to tell others about their bad behavior, then they should have treated us differently.

While there is some truth to that, I would like to add this thought: As a woman of options, I have the freedom and right to tell all. *Yet* I also have the freedom to choose discretion—the right word at the right time.

I think of discretion as the *selah* of relationships. You know how the word *selah* often appears in the Psalms after truth has been declared? The common interpretation is that readers and listeners are being directed to pause. To reflect. To consider what they have just heard before responding. *Selah* is a discretionary sort of action.

There is usually a time and place for the whole story to be told. And that's how it should be. Again, I hope you, as a woman of options, will be discerning about what you share with your daughter and when. Blend truth with grace. Pause and have a *selah* moment wherein you reflect and consider before proceeding.

Dear Robin . . .
When my daughter was fifteen, I heard you talk about doing something special with our daughters before they begin their period. I wish I had heard your talk about five years earlier, because I know it would have meant a lot to my daughter if I had said or done something.

But I decided it wasn't too late, so I thought through all my options based on what means the most to her, and I knew she'd like it if I went out for coffee with her. We started going on Friday afternoons at four o'clock.

The first time we went, I pulled out a magazine and

said I was thinking of getting my hair cut like the woman in the picture. I asked what she thought. She pulled up pictures on her phone and showed me some other styles she thought might look better. One of them I really liked, so I asked her to send it to me so I could show the hairstylist.

She ended up going with me to my appointment because the soonest opening was for the next Friday at four. We bought our coffee first, and she sipped her latte while I got a haircut. I liked how it turned out, and she told everyone that it was her suggestion.

The next Friday I read to her from a novel I was reading that was set in Italy. I liked the vivid description and wanted to share it with her. The next week she brought a project she had been working on in her art class and opened her usually hidden sketchbook so I could see her work.

We have kept this tradition going almost every Friday for the past two years. I know it might sound strange that we live in the same house but had to schedule a coffee date to get to know each other better. Yet it's working. We share little bits of our lives and talk about all kinds of things because it's just the two of us.

On her eighteenth birthday I gave her my present during our Friday coffee date. It was a coupon I'd made for a weekend trip to Seattle and dinner at the Space Needle. I knew it was something she had wanted to do for a long time. Inside the card I wrote that I loved her and was proud of her. Then I wrote, "You are an exceptional woman. I have loved being by your side for the journey into your adult years. I hope you know that I will always be here for you."

We both cried. That was our moment—eye to eye, heart to heart.

I often think that my daughter was at a crossroads when she was fifteen, but we hardly talked about anything personal back then. If you hadn't challenged us as moms to do something special with our daughters, I don't want to think about all that I might have missed!

I told a friend what I've been doing with my daughter, and that prompted her to take horseback-riding lessons with her sixteen-year-old. On a trail ride in the woods last year, her daughter told my friend that she had been waiting and hoping for the day when her mother would start being her friend as well as her mom. The change in their relationship has been amazing.

You're right, Robin. We need to take the first step as moms, and we should never think that it's too late.

Start Now

What are some ways you might put the ideas from this chapter into action? What portions of the chapter stood out to you? Here are some possible points of action:

- Thank God for His mighty power at work in you. Believe that He is able to do far more than you would ever dare ask or even dream.
- Think of the good things that were woven throughout your childhood. Be intentional about recounting those

stories and speaking well of the people who loved you and were kind to you.

- Ask God for the wisdom to know what to say to your daughter about your past—and when to say it.
- Consider how to incorporate discretion into your conversations with your daughter.
- Find ways to connect more with your daughter and start building more bridges.
- Give yourself the freedom and grace to start over— or to start now—in becoming a sheltering tree and affirming voice in your daughter's life.

Notes

before your tween daughter becomes a woman

bring the sacred

This is probably my favorite chapter in the book, because I love it when the eternal is brought into the commonness of life. It enlivens me to spend time thinking and studying concepts that are eternal and then expressing them in ways that are easy to understand.

We are surrounded by the beauty and holiness of the One who created us. What a gift it is to help our daughters see the wonders of God's goodness in the midst of all the horrible things that happen in this world.

What Can I Bring?

A few years ago, some of the women at my church put our heads together to plan a bridal shower for one of our dearly loved college students. My friends described what each of them was going to bring—decorations, a dessert, and so on. We were at the end of the list, but I hadn't jumped in yet.

"What can I bring?" I asked.

"You bring the sacred," replied the hostess. "That's what you do best."

I remember feeling my heart flutter with anticipation. I had the privilege of bringing something to this shower that would elevate it beyond a time of gifts, food, and games. We were gathering to celebrate a sacred event. Two would soon become one in holy matrimony, and as her fellow women, we were launching this young bride into the next season of her life.

I shared a special devotional thought inspired by Bible verses that seemed applicable specifically to the bride-to-be. I teared up a bit (and so did she) as I blessed her. The moment felt to me like a candle had been lit—flickering, warming, and touching all of us in that circle of women. I love bringing the sacred.

Speaking in public would cause some of my friends to lose sleep at the mere thought, but they are the ones who have other gifts—ones I do not possess. They show up with mouthwatering appetizers presented perfectly on heirloom platters. They find the ideal gift and wrap it so beautifully that the guest of honor says she doesn't want to open it and spoil the presentation. They are the ones who willingly step outside the circle of smiles and stories to stand in the corner and listen intently while one of the other guests pours out her heart. A vibrant sacredness is present in all their offerings.

So here's my challenge to you, willing moms: Ask yourself,

what are the gifts that you bring to your daughter, as well as to other women in your circle? Tap into those gifts and explore them fully as you walk side by side with your daughter across the bridge to womanhood.

But don't try to be someone you're not. Your daughter will recognize right away if you attempt to arrange something meaningful that doesn't feel authentic. Whatever you do, make sure it rings true to who you are and where you feel most at home.

If you would never feel comfortable with a teacup in your hand, then don't even consider a tea party. If the great outdoors is where you feel at home, then take her outside for your heart-to-heart conversation. Let her see the delight on your face and feel the wonder of creation—a sense of worship that happens naturally when you gaze up at the sky or reach for an amber leaf on a crisp fall day and twirl it between your fingers.

As I've mentioned already, you certainly want to understand her love language and consider what's most comfortable for her. That's where to begin, because it shows you're making the effort to help her feel at ease—especially if you have an inkling that the first conversation or two might be uncomfortable for her.

Then, as your friendship grows and the conversation continues, invite her into where and how you feel closest to God. Let her share the intimacy of watching you be your truest self.

If music is your sweet spot—or hers—then expand the ways you share that passion. Do you feel closest to God when you're in church? Invite her to sit beside you and be surrounded by all the elements of the service. She might not yet have found her most natural way to connect with God, so help introduce her to more than what she's known through traditional childhood exercises in faith. Include her in broader, more grown-up expressions of worship.

Doing Your Job

A few days ago, a friend who's raising a preteen daughter told me she felt as if she'd been "cut adrift" and was no longer included in what she considered to be the most important parts of her daughter's life.

"What happened?" I asked.

"I knew she was upset about something," she said, "so I did what I always have tried to do: I asked her if she wanted to talk about whatever was bothering her. She shook her head and gave me a look. She said something quietly and walked away. I didn't know what to do."

In a weak attempt to offer comfort, I said, "It's typical at that age, you know."

"I know. But it wasn't as if she was pulling back. Her look wasn't rebellious. It was soft. She didn't stomp off to her room."

"What did she do?"

My friend sighed. "She looked at me with the sweetest expression and said she wanted to go talk to God about everything, and then she would tell me after she had poured out her heart to Him first."

"That's beautiful," I said.

"I know. It's beautiful and mature, and I'm a horrible person because I feel like I'm jealous of God right now."

We laughed softly, the way close friends do.

"You're not a horrible person," I told her. "You are a mom who did a great job of showing your daughter how to go to God with everything, and now that's what she's doing on her own."

"I just wish she wasn't such a fast learner," my friend replied.

We smiled and talked about how quickly children grow and how much they pick up from us. My friend had brought the sacred into her daughter's life, and for all the years ahead, her daughter would know how to keep developing that closeness with God. He would always be there for her and with her—no matter where she went or what happened in her life.

The Story of the Fine China Plate

If you're not sure where to start or how to incorporate a sense of the sacred as your daughter advances on her journey to womanhood, then maybe the following true story will help. The imagery emerged from a real-life moment I experienced with the daughter of my closest friend. It has since become an often-repeated analogy of how to explain the concepts of holiness and sanctification to a child.

Years ago, when my kids were toddlers, they were napping on a summer afternoon while I was in the backyard picking cherries from a tree. I'd filled a bowl and was taking them inside to wash when a friend came by with her nine-year-old daughter, Natalie, and asked if I could keep an eye on her for a few hours.

Natalie was quiet as she watched me pat the cherries dry and dip them in a saucepan of warm chocolate. As I lined up the chocolate cherry treats on waxed paper, I asked her what was wrong.

"It's just not fair," she said. "All my friends went to the movies, but my parents said I couldn't go. They said it wasn't the kind of movie I should see."

Natalie sighed. "My parents are too protective of me," she continued. "They said they wanted me to stay clean. What does that even mean?"

I knew she was eyeing the cherries, and I wanted to share some with her, but I wanted to make it special. Her question sparked an idea.

"Would you like some cherries?" I asked.

"Yes, I would."

I went to the kitchen garbage and pulled out a dirty paper plate stained with beans and hot dogs from the previous night's barbecue.

"You're not going to use that dirty plate, are you?" Natalie asked.

I shrugged, holding the paper plate in my hand, waiting for her to continue.

"Don't you have any other plates to use?"

"Oh, yes." I returned the paper plate to the garbage and went over to the antique hutch. "I have other plates. They're special plates. Clean plates. Plates that I have kept set apart."

Natalie watched as I opened the door and lifted out a single fine china plate. "I'm probably overly protective of these plates," I told her. "They're valuable and beautiful. They were a gift to me and I treasure them, so I want to always keep them clean and ready so that I can use them to serve others."

A flicker of understanding shone in Natalie's eyes. "It's a beautiful plate," she said as I placed it in front of her with the yummy chocolate-covered cherries.

"Yes, it is," I agreed. "And so are you, Natalie. You are more valuable than you can even imagine. God gave you to your parents as a special gift. Don't you see? You've been set apart too."

"That's why they're so protective of me," she said in a low voice. "I'm not a paper plate to them."

"No, you're not. You are a fine china plate, and you've been set apart so that your heart will stay clean, and you'll be ready to serve others with honor and beauty."

Natalie tilted her head. "Did my mom tell you to say all this?"

"No."

"Then where did this come from?"

I smiled because the concept of being set apart wasn't mine, and it wasn't new. It was ancient and had been expressed many times by God in His Word.

"It came from the same place all the best truth comes from— the Bible."

Natalie looked surprised. "I didn't know the Bible said anything about plates."

I went into the other room and came back with my Bible.

"It's right here," I said. "Just listen: 'If you stay away from sin, you will be like one of these dishes made of purest gold— the very best in the house—so that Christ Himself can use you for His highest purposes.'"

I showed her the verse in 2 Timothy 2:21 in *The Living Bible*: "You will be like one of these dishes made of purest gold . . ."

I told Natalie, "Your parents are helping you stay clean in your heart and in your mind by keeping you set apart from things in this world that they believe aren't good for you."

Later that afternoon, when it was time for Natalie to go home, I had a gift for her. I'd written 2 Timothy 2:21 on the back of one of my treasured fine china plates, and I handed it to her with a big smile.

"You are a fine china plate," I told her. "Never forget that."

Natalie hung the plate in a prominent spot on her bedroom wall. As her body, mind, heart, and soul sauntered into her teen years, the plate was a gentle reminder that she was greatly treasured and set apart to stay clean so that Christ could use her for His noble purposes. Many of the choices she made in the years that followed were influenced by the simple conversation we had that summer afternoon.

The impression was lasting because the moment was holy. The conversation focused on God's truth. On His values. On what matters for eternity.

You and I have no idea what might happen when we bring the sacred. I hope we never miss the opportunity to elevate those rare and wonderful moments when God's Spirit inspires us to share truth, hope, and light with our daughters. I hope you'll find joy in bringing a little extra to birthdays, holidays, and one-on-one conversations by looking for the eternal and figuring out your best way to express it.

Initiate a Deeper Conversation

Here are three ways you can bring a more worshipful approach to your ongoing conversation with your daughter:

1. TELL HER SHE WAS WANTED.

Were you elated when you learned you were pregnant with your daughter? Then tell her so. Let her see your smile when you recall how you couldn't wait to get your first ultrasound, to hear her heartbeat. Describe what it was like the first time you felt her fluttering inside and how you sang to your daughter and prayed for her or whatever it was that began between the two of you before you ever saw each other face to face. Tell her how much you loved her before she was even born.

Share with your daughter how in awe you were when she arrived. Or when you first held her. Or how you felt when you began the adoption process and hoped that God would bring her into your life. Talk about how God worked in your life to bring her to you. Tell her that she was wanted then, and she is wanted now.

What you say and the way you say it doesn't have to sound unrealistically mushy or as romantic as I might be making it sound. Just say what's true, and say it from your heart.

2. DEMONSTRATE THE SACRED.

Develop a pattern of praying with your daughter regularly. If praying aloud is still something you're developing in your life, be willing to learn alongside her. Start with simple, honest words. Thank God for what He's given you and done for you. Invite her to say whatever she wants to add to your prayer.

Blessing your children each night is a wonderful pattern to develop. We did this when our kids were young and continued it when they were teens. I still remember those nights when they would head upstairs to bed and call out, "Are you going to come and bless me?" We always answered yes.

It's a privilege to be the one who gets to bless your child at the end of each day. You are the one speaking the name of our heavenly Father over her in a sacred way. Think about how many times a day she might hear God's name spoken in an unsacred way. You are countering this and demonstrating that God is holy.

Consider this: If you don't demonstrate to her how to pray and express a sense of reverence in communicating with God, who will? From what other sources is she seeing what it looks like to have an intimate relationship with her heavenly Father?

3. WORSHIP OPENLY.

For many, worship is a personal experience. When you remain open and share that part of yourself with your daughter, your vulnerability in expressing your spiritual self will encourage her to express her similar feelings with you. Shared worship is a beneficial and much-needed closeness that can help carry the two of you through difficult times in the years ahead. You're teaching her that the inner life is of high value. That connection to the eternal and the freedom to express her heart are essential dimensions of her life.

It has been part of my life rhythm to read my Bible, pray, and journal each week. When our children were young, I sat in my favorite snuggle chair for these quiet times of worship and reflection. On an end table next to the chair, I'd light a candle. My kids knew that if they saw me in that chair, with my Bible open or my head bowed and the candle lit, they were to not interrupt. I was in an important meeting with the King of the universe, and I was probably talking to Him about them! They saw what worship looked like for their mom and learned to respect those sacred moments.

I can almost hear what some of you are thinking right about now. If you've made it this far in the book, you're probably on suggestion overload—perhaps approaching mothering responsibility meltdown. I'm sure your life is busy. You might have multiple children. You likely have responsibilities that require all your energy. Maybe you're still deciding if you're really ready to make peace with your past. Finding a way to do even half the ideas included in this book already sounds like a part-time job, and the thought of going to your daughter's room every night to bless her just about puts you over the edge.

That's okay.

Take a deep breath and ask yourself what really matters the most. If you currently have some obvious time-drainers in your life that don't offer real, lasting value, think about what it would mean if you removed some of those things from your schedule. Your children will only be under your roof for a short time. What can you let go of to make space for a few sacred moments with your daughter?

Dear Robin . . .

After hearing you on the radio, I found a new appreciation for my childhood. My mom didn't grow up going to church and didn't have many Christian influences during her younger years. When I was eight, she and my dad gave their lives to Christ and wanted to raise their children differently than they'd been raised.

I think my mom did a good job figuring out what was important based on what she wished she had been told or given. She bought matching Bibles for my brother and me, and we started a game of trying to find different verses. We would both underline them, and when we went to church and wrote notes in the margins, we would compare what we had learned. It was new to all of us at once, and that made the discoveries fun.

When I was eleven, our family was sitting around the firepit in our backyard on a summer evening. The topic of sex and puberty somehow came up, and my parents talked to my brother and me in a relaxed and open way. I learned everything I really needed to know at that age. I didn't feel uncomfortable at the time, but when I started my period a few months later, I felt really embarrassed and didn't want anyone except my mom to know.

My mom set up a special day for just the two of us and told me it was a "Celebration of Menstruation," which sounded strange to me, but at the same time it made what was happening to my body feel more normal. We went shopping and out to lunch. Throughout the day she said a lot of positive things about how proud she was of me and how she could see God's love in my life.

What I remember most was that when we got home, she reached over and took my hand. She told me I was pretty, smart, and kind. Then she prayed and thanked God for making me and letting her be my mom. It was a lot sweeter than I'm making it sound.

It's one of my favorite memories, because not only did I feel grown-up and included in the world of womanhood, but I also felt like she showed me how God's presence is over everything in life. It was like the natural way that she and my dad talked about sex around the firepit. I knew then that I always wanted to be aware of God's presence. I knew that He was always there, and I wanted to grow closer to Him—the same way that my mom and I were growing closer.

Start Now

What are some ways you might put the ideas from this chapter into action? What portions of the chapter stood out to you? Here are some possible points of action:

- What needs to shift in your schedule for you to invest more in those things that will matter for eternity?
- Think about the things you do well and that bring you joy. How do you see them as a means of sharing what is sacred or using them in an act of worship?

- Where have you held back in letting your daughter learn how you communicate with God and how you're growing in your relationship with Him?
- What can you do to open wider channels between your daughter and you in terms of your spiritual lives?
- What is one simple way you could express to your daughter that God is with her every day and that He loves her?

Notes

bring the sacred

women like us

Have you noticed how your own view of life can change when you realize that other people around the globe are having the same experiences as you? We are not isolated as moms, nor as women. Virtually every woman in the world, from the beginning of time, has experienced menstruation.

When I was fourteen, our family took a trip around the United States in a camper. The three of us kids groaned every time we stopped at another Civil War battlefield site or spent another night parked in the driveway of another relative we had never met before. Yet by the end of our journey, something unexpected had happened.

Our young views and understanding of other people, places, and cultures had expanded.

This happened naturally as we were introduced to a Hopi ceremonial dance in Arizona or were on a tour of Williamsburg, Virginia, where guides in period costumes demonstrated what life was like during the American Revolution.

We connected with many interesting people. One sultry night in Tennessee I chased fireflies with a girl I had just met named Judy. In Texas we swung on a rope over a swimming hole with local kids who owned their own horses. We made s'mores with our campground neighbors in North Carolina. We paddled a canoe on one of Minnesota's ten thousand lakes and listened to our uncle recite Longfellow's epic poem "Hiawatha."

Our family connections became vivid, and distant relatives became familiar. The United States became a living, breathing country—alive with stories, accents, tastes, and sights I never would have understood without exploring beyond Southern California's beach culture.

Cultures and Common Ground

In a similar way, as I was conducting the research for this book, my appreciation for women in other places and cultures expanded. I took a virtual tour throughout history and around the world, learning how a young girl's coming-of-age has been viewed and celebrated in various cultures over the centuries.

I discovered many references to the rituals, chants, and instructions for how a young girl can awaken her inner goddess. Menstruation in some cultures is observed with red foods that aligned the child-turned-woman with the moon, the tides, and her Zodiac sign. Others include prayers to Mother Earth.

These varied entrance-to-womanhood incantations made me wish that more writers who honor God would craft books for both mothers and daughters. I believe women are empowered and aligned when they look beyond the elements of our physical sphere and humbly bow before the One who created them—who created the whole universe! All power and life come from Father God, the One who made heaven and earth.

This is what our daughters need to hear from us many times over, because other voices will always be lurking in the background. When our daughters understand that God made their intricate bodies, and when they believe that He is the giver of life and health and all that makes us distinctly female, their inner strength will grow and be anchored in truth.

As you read about the following global traditions, you might see a connection to your family heritage. Learning more about where the women of your family have come from will give you a better sense of understanding about your mother and grandmother. Not all traditions are included, but you'll see that many of them are based on a sacred foundation.

A Sampling of Global Traditions

Jewish Customs

The first recorded account of Bar Mitzvahs for boys was in France during the Middle Ages. No specific coming-of-age ceremony is referred to in the Old Testament. Details about Bat Mitzvahs for girls can be traced back to the late nineteenth century. It was to be a day of happiness when a daughter would enter the obligation of the Commandments. This occurs when she is twelve or thirteen, depending on whether the family is part of the Orthodox, Conservative, or Reformed Jewish tradition.

Bat Mitzvahs gradually became more lavish affairs that included blessings, feasting, dancing, and a toast by the parents. Usually the father offers thanks to God that he is no longer held responsible for his daughter's sins. The gathering of family and friends at the event demonstrates the support the young girl can rely on and is symbolic of how she is to establish her place in her Jewish community.

High Church Customs

In Catholic, Anglican, Orthodox, and other High Church traditions, both boys and girls are "confirmed" after they have taken their first Communion. The confirmation ceremony signifies a child's "age of accountability," which generally is between eight and twelve years old. Before confirmation, children are prepared to understand and receive their first Communion at a service attended by family and friends.

In some churches girls traditionally don white dresses to represent purity and are crowned with a wreath of flowers. In countries such as Spain, Germany, Luxembourg, and Austria, the young girls are dressed as brides. Boys wear suits in most countries, but in Scotland they wear kilts. In Switzerland both boys and girls wear simple white robes with a wooden cross around their neck.

India

In many parts of India and other predominantly Hindu countries, when a girl has her menarche, she has attained the ability to bear children and her newly blossomed sexuality is celebrated by a grand party called *Ruthu Sadangu* or *Pen Vaisu Vanthachu*. Some communities maintain that the coming-of-age rites must be performed on the day the girl starts her period.

Purifying rituals are performed by women in the extended family, and a time of isolation for the girl is included. This is followed by a large party with gifts and rich foods during which the young woman is adorned with jewels, flowers, and the finest clothing.

Japan

In previous generations, a special dish of sweet mochi rice and red adzuki beans called *sekihan* was served to a Japanese girl when she had her first period. The dish was kept secret from the extended family until it was served, at which point the reason for the special celebration was discreetly understood. Sekihan is still served at special occasions such as birthdays, but the tradition of serving it to mark the menarche is no longer as common.

Latin America

A *quinceañera* is a familiar tradition in Latin American culture during which a girl is symbolically escorted into womanhood by her family when she turns fifteen. The roots are attributed to ancient Aztec ceremonies, but nowadays the grand fiesta usually begins with Mass and is followed by a large party. The young woman, adorned in a fancy dress, usually dances with her father before her mother takes her to a "throne" where a tiara is placed on her head. Her father removes her sandals and slips on her first pair of high heels before leading her back to the dance floor. No longer a child, she is now viewed in her community as a woman.

The Philippines

Many families in this region continue to honor a daughter's eighteenth birthday with a traditional *debut*, which is a celebration of life and what is to come. The ceremony is a formal affair and can be as extravagant as a wedding. It often includes a family procession, a prayer or blessing, and traditional dress. The young woman is honored with the traditional "eighteen treasures," which are meaningful gifts given by eighteen friends who were carefully selected as her event entourage. The gifts demonstrate how well each of the friends know the debutante.

A meaningful father-daughter dance is followed by a birthday cake and a speech by the young woman during which she can express her thoughts on life and her gratitude to her parents, extended family, and friends.

Europe

Debutante (French for "female beginner") is the word that describes young women of high society throughout Europe and the United Kingdom. Movies have depicted many historical images of how young women from aristocratic backgrounds were introduced into society at formal events once they reached maturity. These matchmaking occasions also allowed young women who were old enough to marry to be presented to eligible bachelors from an approved circle.

For several centuries, debutantes in upper circles of British society prepared for the so-called "social season" when they would be presented at court in hopes of being noticed by a suitable bachelor. Queen Elizabeth II abolished the ceremony in 1958, at which point the tradition became increasingly insignificant due to the withdrawal of royal influence.

In Austria, however, the social season continues to thrive from January through March, when twenty-five formal balls are held in Vienna. Carefully selected debutantes glide across the dance floor with enough elegance to keep young girls dreaming of a potential future filled with castles and princes.

Africa

In places like urban Kenya, ancient traditions are changing as the current generation of leaders has implemented various alternative rites of passage programs. Many are conducted through churches and have had a positive effect on the preteen boys and girls who go through the yearlong sessions separately. Often the training culminates with an adventure ceremony, such as climbing Mount Kenya, to both test and celebrate a child's transition into adulthood.

Girls are awarded documents at the end of the ceremony that serve as tangible evidence of their transition from girls to young women. This is vastly different from the diminishing tradition of female circumcision that has long been common in parts of Africa and the Middle East.

Canada

The Nootka tribe on the west coast of Canada is known for placing a high value on a young woman's physical endurance, because it demonstrates that she is ready to face the rigors of motherhood. The rite of passage for girls at the time of their menarche is to be rowed out into the Pacific Ocean, where they enter the frigid water and are expected to swim to shore. The village watches and waits to either congratulate her or to send a rescue party.

The Global Commonality

One mom who wrote to me said her daughter wanted to know about all her options for feminine products when she started her period. The two of them enjoyed online shopping together, so it was natural for them to spend an evening side by side, browsing various sites.

The mom found it easy to explain why various sizes and thicknesses of pads were available, as well as how an applicator works. Their search also brought up an array of related products, so the conversation branched off into a discussion of body odors and the best ways to dispose of used items.

They chose all the essential items during their online shopping spree and added a few other recommended products. When the package arrived, the daughter eagerly awaited the first time she would need to use the pads, whether she started her period at home or at school.

During their online search, they discovered that an estimated five hundred million girls and women globally do not have the adequate resources or knowledge to properly care for themselves during their periods.

A bit more research led the mother and daughter to websites that suggested ways they could serve together to help provide education for women in rural areas outside their community. The pair were motivated to help raise awareness about the lack of supplies and initiated a local donation drive.

Staying Healthy

Many feminine products are now created using natural fibers. They use no plastics and are made without potentially harmful chemicals such as bleach. Have you tried a variety of products? If not, you might want to test out some new options yourself so that when your daughter is ready, you'll be able to offer recommendations. This is especially helpful if you've been using the same product for decades and have nothing to compare it with.

One mom told me she made her own washable pads when she experienced health issues with products from the major manufacturers. Her daughter also wanted her own custom fit pads, so she came up with a variation on her mom's design. The experience was an unexpected opportunity for more discussions and woman-to-woman bonding time.

Include in the conversation with your daughter the topic of

cramps. Try to not dismiss them as simply part of every girl's monthly experience.

One young woman told me how she was diagnosed with a serious health condition after her mom had told her for eight years that the pain was just normal cramps. The daughter had nothing to compare the pain to, and her mother thought she was "being a baby" even though the daughter was doubled over and felt like she was going to pass out. I'm sure the mother felt terrible when she discovered her daughter's level of pain was very real, as was her health issue.

If you have any questions at all about your daughter's health, take her in for a consultation with your family physician. Let your doctor eliminate any potential issues, which can range from endometriosis and cysts to ovarian tumors and cervical cancer. Even if your daughter is told after a round of tests that what she's experiencing are indeed cramps, at least she will have a baseline to know what's normal for her and how to manage the pain.

The other valuable part of such an appointment is that you can help her learn how to express where it hurts and how intense the pain is. Ask your doctor about all the options for pain management rather than accepting the old directive to "take two and call me in the morning." By being your daughter's advocate, you're helping her learn how to express what she feels and demonstrating how to go about obtaining help when she needs it.

After researching this information about past history and other cultures, I felt a greater empathy for what my grandmother and the women before her had to do each month in order to care for themselves hygienically. I also saw why so much secrecy and unspoken disdain was linked to menstruation. These insights gave me even more reason to release and move past the residual hurts from my childhood. The women in my family had plenty of company in avoiding any potentially uncomfortable conversations with their daughters.

So let's eliminate the stigma for our daughters and equip them to have a healthy, reverent, and grateful perspective regarding their bodies. What a beautiful change it would be if young women paused to be thankful and whispered an honest prayer at their menarche by saying, "Thank you, God, for making me a woman and for blessing my body this way."

It begins with you, dear moms.

Dear Robin . . .
I wanted to tell you my story because I thought you might like to hear how the women from my culture responded to my entrance into puberty. I didn't begin to develop until I was thirteen, yet as soon as my mother noticed, she made me start wearing loose-fitting tops and told me that "Ama," my grandmother, would be coming from Taiwan for an important visit. I had only seen my grandmother three times, so I was excited. I didn't realize that I *was the reason for her long journey until I saw the wrapped gifts in her suitcase. She said all of them were for me, but I couldn't open them until we had our tea and* Yue Bing *(also known as "moon cakes").*

Moon cakes are round pastries that have a thin crust and different kinds of fillings. Ama brought some moon cakes with mung bean paste and others with green tea filling.

The next afternoon, when I came home from school, the dining room table was set with china plates and teacups. A plate of the promised moon cakes and a pot of expensive oolong tea were in the center of the table, and all the gifts were waiting by my seat. Ama was at the head of the table and had on a beautiful red silk brocade top. She quoted a poem or saying in Taiwanese, and we drank the tea and ate the moon cakes in silence. My mom and Ama kept smiling at me.

I was finally told I could open the presents, and they explained that these were gifts for a woman, not a child. I unwrapped pretty things like simple pieces of jewelry, a scarf, and a fancy pen. Ama said the gifts were from the women relatives in my family, each of whom had been given these gifts when they left childhood.

That's when I began to understand what the ceremony was all about. I had picked up enough details about the facts of life over the years, and I was old enough to feel comfortable with all the unspoken elements of the gentle, solemn, private ceremony. I liked feeling that I was now included with the women in my family. I told my Ama how honored I was that she had come all the way to our home at this time in my life.

I have no idea if what my mom and grandma did

for me was specifically linked to our Taiwanese culture, or if it was something developed over the years between the women in my extended family. The tradition lives on, though, because I have a second cousin in Canada whose daughter will be twelve this year. My cousin asked if I would be willing to share one of my "woman's gifts" for the upcoming tea party she was planning. I've saved all the presents I received and decided to send a porcelain butterfly pin. I think I'll include a note and tell her daughter to spread her wings and fly into adulthood.

Start Now

What are some ways you might put the ideas from this chapter into action? What portions of the chapter stood out to you? Here are some possible points of action:

- Research your family heritage and culture and share with your daughter what you learned about those customs.
- Keep up a family tradition, or start a new one with the women in your family.
- If your daughter enjoys history, let her research your family tree and invite her to share her findings in a way that feels most comfortable to her—at the family dinner table, alone with you, or in a written report that can serve double duty as a homework assignment or extra-credit project.
- Try a recipe connected to your family heritage. Include your daughter in the preparation of the traditional food and add other cultural touches, such as learning some

words in a language that your great-grandparents spoke or listening to music specific to their culture.

- Use discussions of your family heritage as a chance to instill respect for other cultures. Elevate your daughter's understanding of what it means to honor others while retaining your own foundational culture, traditions, and sacred beliefs.

Notes

before your tween daughter becomes a woman

my hope for you

I hope this book has given you freedom from the chains of your past; shame off you, grace on you. I hope you have drawn closer to God and felt a new sense of gratitude knowing that He created you exactly the way He did and made you a beautiful woman.

I also hope this book enables you to do something—anything—that will show the daughter in your life that you esteem her, are there for her, and deeply love her.

I hope you pray for your daughter more than you ever have before. We can't fully grasp the power that prayer has in the unseen world. What we do know is that God has healed relationships in amazing ways, prodigal daughters have returned home, and women have successfully managed, through prayer, not to turn out "just like their mother."

So keep praying. For yourself, for your daughter, and for the two of you together.

Another of my hopes is that you will learn the fine art of

dreaming *alongside* your daughter rather than dreaming *for* her. That way you'll be able to celebrate together when her dreams come true.

My final hope for you is that you'll understand at a heart level who you are in Christ. I've included a poem from my journal that I wrote for my daughter as I watched her be an amazing mom to her children. It's titled "More Than," and it first appeared in a small gift book I wrote called *A Pocketful of Hope for Mothers.*

May there be many meaningful conversations between your daughter and you, for many years to come. And may the next generation and generations far beyond reap the rich rewards of the efforts you make to honor and celebrate your daughter when you welcome her into womanhood.

"more than"

a poem for my daughter

I was wrong.
 My darling daughter, I was wrong.
I told you that you were enough.
 Enough woman, mother, chef, teacher, puppeteer . . .
Today I saw the deeper truth as I watched you accomplish
 heroic acts of everyday motherhood.
 Now I know that you are not enough.
 No.
The truth is . . .
 you are more than.
More than
 the length of your days
 or the breadth of your knowledge.

More than
    yesterday's accomplishments
    or tomorrow's goals.
You are more than you were when you started this journey
    into motherhood.
More than
    a diaper-changing station
    or a twenty-four-hour concession stand.
You are more than you can see;
    more than your thin emotions can feel.
You are more than the sum of all your parts.
    More than what you saw in the mirror this morning.
    More than what you told yourself three minutes ago.
Listen. Hear this and treasure it in your heart.
You don't have to
    do more
    be more
    give more
    try more.
You already are more.
    More than you know.
You are
    a song in the night
    a gentle touch
    a calm word
    an assuring smile
    a soft kiss.

"more than"

You are not just enough, dear little mama.
  You are more than.
In all things, for all days,
you are more than a conqueror through Him who
  handcrafted you
  unfailingly loves you
  continually guides you.
He is the One who placed on you the care of these eternal
    souls—
  the Giver of all good gifts.
The One who is
  and was
  and is to come.
He will give you more than enough to see you through.

ROBIN JONES GUNN

parenting is about preparation

Conversations are like a dance. Some are a little or a lot smoother than others. My hope is that Robin's book has inspired you to initiate some potentially difficult introspection and some intentional life-giving conversations with your daughter—to begin and continue the dance. Did you know conversations have the power to line up your brain with your daughter's brain, and to deeply influence you—even your breathing? (Have you ever noticed the need to take a deep breath after a difficult conversation with your daughter?)

Did you know the average person takes up to twenty breaths a minute? That's about twelve hundred per hour. I'm pretty sure there are some situations that have pushed me well beyond that number per hour, including this recent conversation:

"Dad, did you get my text?" my daughter said. "I got asked out today! I said no."

I'll be honest, my breathing rate probably increased a bit

as I pondered the thought of my daughter dating. We talked about it at the dinner table that night. We were going to create a dating contract when she turned sixteen, but she said she was waiting until seventeen or eighteen and was not in any hurry to date boys. She had seen the tiring and confusing dating drama unfold all around her. In this particular "just-asked-out" case, she heard that this young man asked several girls out at a mall a few weeks before he asked her, so she was not at all interested.

But my thoughts persisted: *Is she really ready for all this? Will the young men who pursue my daughter be "consumers" or "contributors"? In other words, will it be all about themselves or about truly loving and wanting the best for her? Will she be a contributor or a consumer as she learns to love another person? Will my daughter be able to enter moments like these with the confidence and understanding that she's a child of God?*

And most important of all: *Have her mom and I prepared her as a young woman?*

In my more than two decades of counseling practice, I have seen what unfortunate results can result from a lack of preparation and intentionality in a young woman's life. Countless mixed messages, desires, and pressures compete for her attention, all of which require significant discernment. Think about what competes for the real estate in your mind. Consider what is happening in and around you and how that impacts the way you respond to what's happening in and around your children. Does it prompt you to have more empathy for your daughter?

I refer to this competitive dynamic as part of life's *momentums*. These momentums are everywhere, and they feel relentless in not only our own lives but also in the lives of our children. They include culture, disagreements, influencers, rumors of wars, news, gossip, music, movies, beliefs, words, social media, emotions, thoughts, sports, relationships, perceptions, and—an especially big one—the past. Momentums are a part of our everyday lives. We're either driven by momentums, countering momentums, or we're causing them. The Holy Spirit, for example, has an overarching momentum. Imagine what it's like to be a Christian youth in today's divided and confused culture—trying to discern the Holy Spirit's leading in the middle of all the noise!

I remember a few years ago when my daughter and I took some time away from all the pressures and noise surrounding us. We went to the mountains of California with a group of other dads and their teens and young adults. We climbed, we backpacked, we rappelled, and, best of all, we had intentional conversations throughout the trip.

I had some time to ponder my past and the impact of that past on my role as a father. I thought about the many opportunities I have to influence my daughter's understanding and management of her relationships, mental health, sexuality, spiritual growth, and everyday decision-making—including her use of technology and use of entertainment. What an incredible gift! This time away was an incredible moment for self-reflection, self-awareness, and focus. It was also a great opportunity to reset and realign with God's momentum.

My daughter and I talked about our relationship, her friendships, her worries, her thoughts, her beliefs, and much more.

We sat side by side as we surveyed the beautiful landscape, with getting to know each other better our only priority. We considered the direction of our lives and our special relationship as father and daughter.

I will never forget reading a word of blessing aloud over my daughter in those California mountains, then watching other dads proclaim words of blessing over their children. I now see why the practice of blessing was both common and desired in Scripture (see Numbers 6; Ephesians 3; 2 Thessalonians 3). For my daughter's blessing, I thought about what I wanted for her future. I said, "May you . . ." several times throughout my words to her. I had to really consider my hopes for my daughter. It prompted me to think about my part in the momentum I want for my daughter's life. A momentum centered on Christ and full of life.

I will also never forget the words of encouragement my daughter wrote to me. Her words were life-giving to my soul, as I believe that mine were to hers. Keep in mind that deep, heart-to-heart conversations with our kids may feel intimidating and difficult at first, but those conversations are rich with opportunity. So have them—imperfections and all!

It's all part of *preparing* our children for the future, which is why I'm excited to know that you chose to read this important book by Robin Jones Gunn. She offers many takeaways and ideas for personal reflection and growth. Through her material, you've gotten to consider how momentums from your past can have a profound impact on your relationship with your daughter. In fact, the momentums in your thoughts, emotions, memories, experiences, and perceptions can greatly influence your ability to listen and learn what your daughter needs, both in the moment and for her future. Robin also offers many practical ideas for guiding your daughter in her journey to womanhood. Lean in. It doesn't all have to be perfect; you just need to be intentional and present.

Did you know that as a mom you have the awesome opportunity and ability to help regulate your child's nervous system with your melodic voice? In fact, researchers say that when you're in a calm place emotionally, that's when *your* voice (and not a dad's voice, no matter how melodic) has the capability to help calm your child's nerves. That's amazing! But your impact extends far beyond that. You provide the guidance and affection that is unique to the mother-daughter relationship.

How intentional are you? How *prepared* are you for your daughter to become a woman? How prepared is your daughter? We tend to do well in preparing for meals, speeches, sporting events, tests, trips, guests, shopping, and many other things, but what about preparing our children for the foundational roles of man or woman?

Robin has done a great job of providing a template for preparing your daughter for womanhood. That includes you pursuing mental and emotional health in your own role as mom. This book is an invitation, and what happens next is up to you and the Holy Spirit. Will you consistently engage with your daughter by investing in her identity as a child of God, and in her faith, hope, and love in the years ahead?

At Focus on the Family, we believe that healthy parents

can lead to thriving children, which results in healthy (and imperfect!), life-giving families. It begins with looking inward and growing as a parent, and with depending wholeheartedly on Jesus. With that momentum, you get to intentionally build up your children as you help influence your family toward a life-giving life in Christ.

Several years ago, as I worked with Christian parents in search of solutions for their children's issues, I began to explore the traits that would provide parents with a helpful, biblical framework for their families. I have found that when parents work diligently on themselves, the outcomes are better not only in their children's decision-making and behaviors but also in improved health and relationships among the family members.

Young women are often deeply influenced by what others think of them. They are bombarded by comparisons and riddled with insecurities. They long to be accepted and wanted by their peers.

This is why it's extremely vital for daughters to have emotionally healthy parents as trusted guides amid the social and emotional chaos that is so common at this stage. And that's why the traits of effective parenting that I compiled include high levels of warmth and sensitivity balanced with high levels of guidance and healthy boundaries. Research affirms that every one of these traits can have a profound and positive impact on a parent's relationship with his or her children and on the children's decisions and behaviors. (I eventually wrote a book called *Seven Traits of Effective Parenting*.)

Here is how these seven traits could play out as you follow

up on what you have learned from reading Robin's book: *Adaptability* is about having the flexibility of mind to adjust to your daughter's personality, decisions, and needs. *Respect* helps you listen well and be a healthy, life-giving presence in your daughter's life. *Intentionality* is all about initiating important interactions with your daughter as you guide her toward a thriving life in Christ.

The fourth trait, *steadfast love*, involves you loving your daughter with all her imperfections and frustrations as she tries to manage peer pressure, hormones, thoughts, hurts, emotions, and the many other challenges that come with being a teenager. *Boundaries and limits* are the consistent and trustworthy rails needed for maturity and growth. *Grace and forgiveness* are necessary to reestablish connection when things don't go well. And *gratitude* helps you maintain a positive mindset that views each day as a new invitation to love and guide your daughter as a child of God.

I can still picture my wife and daughter working through a program called Launch Into the Teen Years—a resource from Focus on the Family created to, just as the name indicates, help parents prepare their preteens for the teenage years. Launch Into the Teen Years includes videos to watch ahead of each lesson. The program includes engaging clips for parent and child to watch together and discuss openly. The resource also helps guide discussions about identity, friendships and relationships, influences, male and female differences, their developing bodies, and the beauty and sacredness of sexuality. What if your daughter were equipped with self-confidence, humility, self-control,

afterword

and empathy? The answer is that she can be, but these traits are developed intentionally, not accidentally.

I was very excited to see my wife investing her time as she went through each video and conversation session with my daughter. Like many preteens, my daughter had some good laughs along the way, along with some awkward and uncomfortable moments to navigate. Launch Into the Teen Years is part of Focus on the Family's ongoing commitment to provide you as parents with the biblically based and practical tools you need to intentionally guide your daughter toward healthy relationships, maturity, and growth in Christ.

As you surely know, you only get to *control* you, and you only get to *influence* your children. Even though you can't prepare your daughter for everything, you can do your best to equip her to be deeply rooted in faith as she faces the pressures and unexpected situations that come her way. Consider spending some time with the *Seven Traits of Effective Parenting* as a starting point, then check out Launch Into the Teen Years when your children reach the appropriate age. Focus on the Family also offers many other practical resources, including FocusOnParenting.com. Most of all, we want to help you guide your children toward a thriving and life-giving faith in Christ.

Dr. Daniel Huerta
VICE PRESIDENT OF PARENTING AND YOUTH,
FOCUS ON THE FAMILY

Books by
Robin Jones Gunn
that your daughter will love

The bestselling Christy Miller series

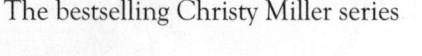

Praying For Your
Future Husband

Before You Meet Your
Future Husband

Learn more at www.RobinGunn.com

FOCUS ON THE FAMILY®

INTO THE

◄ **TEEN YEARS** ►

RELATIONSHIPS. PUBERTY. "THE TALK."

Not sure how to discuss these with your daughter? We've got you. Tackle topics like identity, dating, and more with *Launch Into the Teen Years*.

The video-based lessons will give you and your daughter a biblical foundation for adolescence. *Launch Into the Teen Years* comes with a parent guide, a journal for your daughter, questions, activities, and helpful tips. Your daughter will learn about these topics from someone – make sure she learns the truth from you!

LEARN MORE:

Help your teen grow her faith in Jesus!

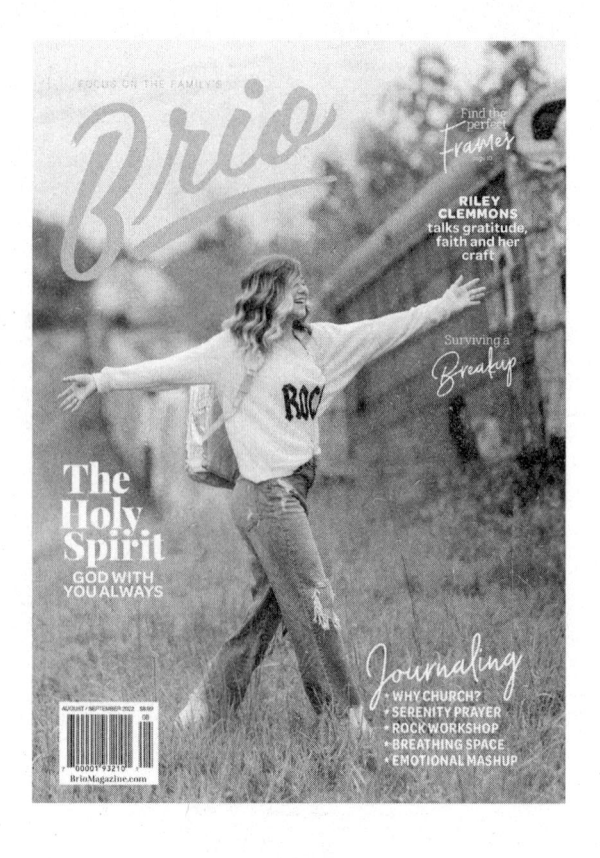

Brio delivers what your teen girl wants to read—entertainment, health, and beauty ideas—and affirms the values you've taught her. Every issue features interactive activities, faith journaling pages, and inspiring practical articles on today's issues.

BrioMagazine.com